ISBN Number 0-8141-1925-5
NCTE Stock Number 19255
Copyright 1965
National Council of Teachers of English
1111 Kenyon Road, Urbana, Illinois   61801

A GUIDE FOR EVALUATING STUDENT COMPOSITION

Readings and Suggestions
for the
Teacher of English
in the
Junior and Senior High School

Prepared for the NCTE by

SISTER M. JUDINE, I.H.M.
Marian High School
Birmingham, Michigan

NATIONAL COUNCIL OF TEACHERS OF ENGLISH

NATIONAL COUNCIL OF TEACHERS OF ENGLISH

READERS OF THE MANUSCRIPT

Edward B. Jenkinson, Director, English Curriculum Center
Indiana University

Jean A. Wilson, Supervisor of Secondary English
Oakland Public Schools, Oakland, California

COMMITTEE ON PUBLICATIONS

James R. Squire, NCTE Executive Secretary, chairman
Jarvis E. Bush, Wisconsin State University—Oshkosh
Glenn Leggett, University of Washington
Virginia M. Reid, Oakland Public Schools, California
Enid M. Olson, NCTE Director of Publications

PUBLICATIONS ON EVALUATION OF COMPOSITION AVAILABLE FROM NCTE

Classroom Practices in Teaching English, 1972-73: Measure for Measure. 06838. $2.45.

The Measurement of Writing Ability. College Entrance Examination Board. 30895. $2.95.

Suggestions for Evaluating Junior High School Writing. Association of English Teachers of Western Pennsylvania. 48980. $2.15.

Suggestions for Evaluating Senior High School Writing. Association of English Teachers of Western Pennsylvania. 49073. $2.45.

(These publications are available at the prices listed from the National Council of Teachers of English, 1111 Kenyon Road, Urbana, Illinois 61801. Please enclose remittance with order of less than $1.00; a $.60 billing charge will be added to all billed orders.)

FOREWORD

This bulletin is intended for high school teachers of English. In it, many teachers and writers discuss the complex factors which must be taken into constant consideration by teachers and lay readers engaged in the correcting of student themes and the general upgrading of the writing practice.

Writing, as one author puts it, involves "the housing of all the most secret resources of the human mind, the consciously acquired furniture of learning and experience, and the special and peculiar thing that is personality, in an inexplicably unique structure that is original expression." No mode, therefore, through which it has passed can be neglected in the evaluation of it. It is for this reason that no consideration of style alone, nor of content within an organized, unified whole, nor of grammatical correctness as the only end to be attained suffices to label the theme a success or failure.

As with every other field, English, too, has its experts. This bulletin presents a cross section of them — some semanticists, some structural linguists, a few philosophers and "pure" critics — all of them teachers, i.e., counselors in the art of communication. Each is concerned that truth be served and that personality be preserved. Each points up definitive and practical means for improving the quality of theme writing while at the same time warning of the psychological effects consequent on overmarking and unreasonable demands for revision.

For reasons of convenience, the bulletin has been divided into sections which concern (1) the writer in relation to his audience, (2) the evaluator's problems and some possible solutions, and (3) the total writing process from its incipiency to its return to the student. We offer the final section (4) as a kind of working "practicum" — particularly for the beginning teacher; it consists of sample assignments and themes containing critical comments which have been assembled from various English classes throughout the nation. The problem of selectivity played a major part in the patterning; however, it is hoped that the inclusion of junior high and senior high school themes may offer some help to teachers in each division.

ACKNOWLEDGMENTS

The committee thanks all authors who contributed their articles to this publication, the editors of journals in which articles appeared originally, and the NCTE affiliates who furnished their guides for evaluating secondary school compositions. Specific credit for each reprinted article is in a footnote on the first page of the article.

CONTENTS

INTRODUCTION

During recent years, concern about the teaching of writing in our schools has led to widespread restudy of instructional programs in composition. This concern has brought about experimental programs for teaching rhetoric and writing, much educational research, and the development of new ideas for teaching materials. Much of the concern has resulted in vigorous attempts to achieve a greater professional consensus on what constitutes good writing.

Repeatedly we have seen demonstrations that teachers of English do not agree on basic standards of excellence in writing. A "B" theme in one English class may earn a "C" or an "A" in another. One recent investigation reported an average disagreement among teachers of as much as seven points on a nine point scale. The reasons for the present confusion are many, not the least being the tendency of each teacher to stress different qualities of writing as he evaluates student papers. In a recent study, Paul B. Diederich, John W. French, and Sydell T. Carlton reported, for example, that theme readers tend to stress five different factors — content, organization, diction, style (or flavor), and mechanics — but that some readers either ignore or overstress one or more of these factors. Many high school teachers of English were found to read for mechanical errors and for very little else. Until teachers are in greater agreement on what they are reading papers for, we cannot expect them to achieve more reasonable sequence in instruction from year to year.

In an attempt to encourage more uniform standards, as well as a more careful consideration of all factors involved in writing ability, teachers in such states as Kentucky, Illinois, Indiana, Pennsylvania, Michigan, and California have prepared statements of recommended practices in composition evaluation. Many of these recommendations have been published by state and regional English associations; a few have been distributed nationally. Believing that the crucial considerations emerging from this recent activity should be made more available to teachers everywhere, the Executive Committee of the National Council of Teachers of English authorized the preparation of a book of selected readings. The Council is fortunate that Sister M. Judine, I.H.M., has been willing to review and organize the readings so that many of the critical problems emerge more clearly than ever before.

The present collection of essays and excerpts raises problems which need to be resolved by every teacher of English. While the collection presents no uniform standard, it suggests how greater uniformity may be achieved. It suggests further some approaches to composition correction which are all too seldom considered in many classrooms — pupil reading of their own themes, use of the overhead projector, selective commenting on individual writing. Included in this book, also, are models of papers annotated by teachers in several states — models for analysis and discussion by teacher groups, not standards to be emulated without careful thought. If used as the stimulus to achieving a greater professional consensus, this collection should provide a helpful basis for reading and lively discussion in departmental meetings, workshops, institutes, as well as in college courses.

September, 1964

JAMES R. SQUIRE
Executive Secretary
National Council of Teachers of English
Professor of English
University of Illinois

THE AUDIENCE: For Whom Does the Student Write?
      "Linguistic Science and Teaching Composition" by S. I. Hayakawa
      "Eleven Common Sense Principles about Language" and "Student Writing Examined for Logic and Clarity" by Irwin Berger
      "Coordinating Composition in High School and College" by Alfred H. Grommon

The first four essays deal with the question: Who is the student's audience? S. I. Hayakawa feels that students should write for each other — not for the teacher. Irwin Berger states they should write for the "Intelligent Stranger" and must, therefore, develop a "sophisticated awareness of words." Alfred Grommon takes for granted that they write for an instructor personally well versed in the art of writing and mindful of college standards in composition.

S. I. Hayakawa dwells on the need for knowledge of "linguistic decorum" in order that the student may communicate effectively to the specific audiences he will eventually meet in the world outside the classroom. The author observes that "if a little of the scientific practice of investigating regional differences of dialect were introduced to the student, he would begin to discover which of his locutions are limited to specific classes or localities and which are more generally accepted."

Mr. Berger supplies practical application to Hayakawa's theory. In a series of eleven principles, he suggests specific means for defining and clarifying terms; he examines faulty theme topic sentences and suggests thoughtful procedures for improving them.

Theory and the writing practice blend in Mr. Grommon's statement of criteria for judging themes according to college standards. With the emphasis on compositions which grow from "judicious" or logical thinking, Mr. Grommon offers some practical suggestions for teaching students to think. He recommends that writing relate to the literature course, and he indicates ideas for essays of this kind.

This article, taken from: Etc: A Review of General Semantics (Winter 1950), laments the tension which many Americans undergo daily "with respect to the use of their own language." The author sees as the basis for this "malaise" the outmoded practice of memorizing endless "prescriptive rules of traditional grammar" which must be carefully applied in formal or even semiformal situations.

As with some other articles in the bulletin, Hayakawa's remarks refer to freshman college classes; their import, however, reaches to all levels of teaching — from grade one to twelve and beyond. He implies that the good speaker or writer is . . . "one who speaks or writes . . . with more than one level of usage at his command and with a trained capacity to observe other kinds of usage. . . ." He states further that such a power enables one "to adjust to many kinds of social and emotional situations" and "to find his own way as he goes along. . . ."

The remainder of the paper follows:

LINGUISTIC SCIENCE AND TEACHING COMPOSITION°

S. I. HAYAKAWA

It appears to me that the usual freshman English theme is bad not because the student is ignorant, but because "writing a theme" is, as normally practiced today, an impossible and artificial communicative situation. The freshman has to write a paper, sometimes on a subject not of his own choosing, often with little assurance that his reader is at all interested in what he has to say, and always with the knowledge that whatever he writes is going to be met with a hostile and critical eye bent on detecting not only his errors of fact or opinion (which he might conceivably correct) but his errors of spelling and grammar and diction, which are judged by a set of rules which appear to him (as they do to more learned students of language) entirely arbitrary and capricious. If you are talking to someone who intently studies the movements of your Adam's apple instead of listening to what you have to say, you will become so uncomfortable and self-conscious that you will soon find yourself stammering.[1] Most freshman themes are written under equally trying conditions, namely, in the knowledge that the incidental and even unconscious mechanics of the communicative act are going to be much more closely attended to than the content. No wonder then, that the average freshman writes uneasily and self-consciously. I venture to say that more than half the errors that we redpencil in composition exercises are not errors of

---

°From S. I. Hayakawa, "Linguistic Science and Teaching Composition," *Etc: A Review of General Semantics*, VII (Winter 1950). Used by permission of S. I. Hayakawa.

[1]See Chapter XVII, "The Indians Have No Word for It: The Problem of Stuttering," in Wendell Johnson's *People in Quandaries* (New York: Harper and Row, 1946), in which the fear of stuttering is shown to give rise to stuttering.

ignorance, but errors of unnaturalness, self-consciousness, and artificiality, arising from the distrust of their *Sprachgefuehl* which has been induced in them by their previous instruction in English.

My main suggestion is, then, that students in freshman English write, not for the teacher, but for each other. Fortunately, dittoing machines and opaque projectors make it easy for students to read each others' themes. The merits of a theme should be judged, not by the teacher, but by classmates, with the teacher acting only as chairman. Disputed usages should be disputed by the class, with the teacher doing no more than providing such background concepts as the determination of correctness by the observation of usage, the different levels of usage, the differences between spoken and written English, and the differences in degrees of formality demanded by different social situations.

Another basic notion that should be employed is the semantic distinction between the two major functions of language. Language first of all communicates something; secondly, through idiosyncrasies of grammar, spelling, diction, or pronunciation, it reveals something about the social status of the speaker. The former is by far the more important function of language, of course, since the content of a statement is the purpose of most communications. Students should be given complete freedom to make their own evaluations of the merit of the content of a paper. If a theme giving instructions on how to clean the ignition points of an automobile enables a reader to perform the process, the communication must be regarded as a success, even if the spelling, punctuation, and grammar are considerably short of "standard." The student will be found to be a better judge than the teacher of the success of a communication by this criterion.

This kind of communicative success is rarely recognized by English teachers, or recognized too fleetingly to do the student any good. Engineering and technical students often write papers that communicate adequately in this sense, but they are so often given low grades for mechanical errors that they come away with the conviction that they "cannot write." This conviction, of course, makes ensuing papers even more difficult for the student. Few English teachers seem to realize that if, as the result of reading a student paper, a reader who couldn't clean ignition points is enabled to do so, the essential purpose of communication has been already accomplished, and that the remaining concerns of grammar, spelling, and punctuation are largely a matter of the proper cutting and placing of the paper panties on one's mutton chop.

But the success of the content of a paper immediately raises, in the student's mind no less than in the teacher's, problems of linguistic propriety. Publication, even the modest form of publication made possible by a projector or dittoing machine, *automatically* brings into play the student's new feeling for the need for some kind of linguistic decorum. I have found that students fear the ridicule and censure of their classmates far more than they fear low grades from a teacher. In trying to solve for himself the problems of linguistic decorum, a student may begin systematically to observe the usage among people of different social levels in his own community and the usages he finds among the newspapers, magazines, and books he has contact with. As students begin to compare and discuss the different standards of propriety in the different social classes and linguistic contexts they encounter, it can be suggested by the teacher that the students work out their own manual of style, appropriate to their own writing situation in the college English class. For this purpose, the teacher may serve as a guide, but not as a lawmaker. A variety of handbooks giving conflicting rulings should be made available to students so that they may choose the forms that seem to them most appropriate.

Sometimes, inevitably, students will arrive at a ruling that differs from standard literary practice: let us suppose that a class decides by majority vote to eliminate the apostrophe from "don't" as a uniform practice in their themes. This will do no harm, for no student who takes part in that decision will be unaware thereafter of the fact that some people believe the word should have an apostrophe, and each will be able to decide, depending on the writing situations he encounters, whether or not to use it.

As an aid in developing the capacity for linguistic observation it might be well to create a very much modified and adapted form of the linguistic atlas questionnaire by means of which the student can investigate the actualities of popular speech in his own class and geographic area.[2] The usual result of English instruction, especially in immigrant, lower class, and Negro areas, is to leave the student feeling that he shouldn't speak the way he does and can't speak the way he ought to. If, however, even a little of the scientific practice of investigating regional differences of dialect were introduced to the student, he would begin to discover, almost without being told, which of his locutions are limited to specific classes or localities and which are more generally accepted. With that knowledge there also arises the curiosity as to what the range of alternative locutions for particular meanings might be. Instead of being left to feel, as he often is now, that the only way to linguistic salvation is to memorize incomprehensible rules which, even when learned, are impossible to apply, the student gets from this training in observation the feeling that he can learn other dialects of English (including those more socially acceptable than his own) by listening and observing closely enough.

A reorganization of freshman composition such as I have sketched will, I believe, make the writing of themes a more natural exercise in communication than it is now. In ordinary life, our communications stand or fall by the judgment of our readers. The good writer is one who can predict accurately the semantic reactions of his readers so that they laugh when he intends them to laugh, are touched when he intends them to be touched. The poor writer is one who cannot predict the reactions of his readers so that they laugh in the wrong places and fail to be touched at all. In the traditional theme writing exercise, the theme is written only for and read only by the instructor, and the student

---

[2]The Linguistic Atlas of the United States and Canada is a large-scale research project into geographical differences in dialect among English-speaking people in America. Most of the inquiries into vocabulary and pronunciation are conducted by questionnaire. See Hans Kurath, *A Word Geography of the Eastern United States* (Ann Arbor: University of Michigan Press, 1949).

writer is expected to write well without having the education or background to be able to predict his reader's semantic reactions. But if the student writes for his fellow students, he writes for a known audience. When his fellow students discuss nis paper in class, he can observe the respects in which he has failed to produce the desired effects, and he can make the necessary changes. Also under such a system he shares in the process of determining the rules for linguistic propriety; the teacher and the handbook become sources of information and guidance and cease to be authorities from on high.[3]

I should go so far as to recommend that the grading be done by students. The last time I made this suggestion publicly, I remember the grim fervor with which an elderly lady English teacher cried, "Never!" I was reminded of common reactions toward proposals that disturbed and delinquent children be treated by progressive, psychiatric methods. When the methods are described — self-government among the children, minimum adult direction, the abolition of adult-imposed punishment — the usual response of the psychologically naive is to say, "Never! Not with the little hoodlums we have to deal with!" But no matter how bad the little hoodlums are, as modern psychotherapists are demonstrating, children even of the seriously disturbed kind are able to socialize each other and develop among themselves self-government and self-discipline. The desire for linguistic propriety, which is only part of a more general desire to be acceptable to one's community, must be seen to be a natural growth development. However, this natural tendency towards linguistic growth is inhibited and subverted, as is the process of socialization among neurotic children, by anxieties and fears. Our profession, with its authoritarian methods and (so far as the majority of us still is concerned) its two-valued prescriptions of linguistic good and evil, is the chief instrument by means of which linguistic anxieties and fears are created and perpetuated — anxieties and fears which leave a large portion of our population frightened of their mother tongue.

Those who share the views on usage of modern linguistics have long deplored the fact that their scientific opinions seem difficult, often impossible, to translate into practical classroom terms. This is not only because, as Professor Paul Roberts recently remarked, the great majority of English teachers still seem to believe that correct English is the joint product of God, Reason, and Richard Grant White. It is also because the structure of the traditional theme assigning and theme writing situation puts English teachers, in spite of themselves, into the role of authorities, so that the demand for authoritarian pronouncements continues unabated in spite of the fact that many of them, as linguistic scientists, hold thoroughly unauthoritarian views on "correct usage." With a change in the structure of the theme writing situation — and I have suggested only one of many

---

[3] The reader acquainted with current trends in psychology will hardly fail to notice, I am sure, the degree to which the point of view presented here coincides with the theories of "nondirective" or "self-directive" counseling (and teaching) proposed by Carl R. Rogers and his associates, and with the theories of group instruction now being tested by the Research Center for Group Dynamics at the University of Michigan. I am indebted to both these schools of thought for sharpened insights into the learning process.

possible changes — the concepts of modern linguistic science will have a chance to operate in composition courses.

English composition is a necessary course in any high school or college curriculum. It will become a vital and more useful course when the tasks it requires and the ways of evaluating success in the performance of those tasks bear a closer resemblance than they now do to the conditions under which writing is produced and evaluated in the world outside the classroom. If the student is trained, in such ways as I have suggested, in linguistic observation; if he is not alienated from his *Sprachgefuehl;* if the course of training he receives increases his confidence in his ability to solve his own linguistic and stylistic problems as they arise, we send him out into the world equipped with the orientation he needs to become a good writer or speaker. Such encouragement of self-guidance and self-maturation seems to me to be psychologically sound as well as consistent with the principles of scientific linguistics.[4]

---

[4]Some teachers on hearing this paper have remarked that the foregoing proposals, while probably useful with advanced composition classes, could hardly be applied to poorer students. Actually, the teaching techniques here described were evolved specifically to meet the problems presented by the poorer students of the kind found in "remedial writing," "subfreshman," and "repeater" sections of the college freshman English course.

In one freshman English course I know of, it was felt some years ago that the students "weren't learning to write." It was decided, therefore, to "drill them in fundamentals" of grammar, spelling, and the like, and to give up fancy notions such as the study of the modern novel, the Great Books, or semantics. After a few semesters of "fundamentals," it was discovered that the students still "weren't learning to write" — in fact, the condition seemed to be getting worse. It therefore seemed apparent that the students had to be drilled in *even more fundamental* fundamentals. But still the students turned in miserable themes.

In the course of a decade, the freshman English course at this institution has become more and more and more elementary, until it is now at about the level of the sixth grade. I keep wondering what the outcome will be. Will they eventually give up the teaching of composition as a bad job? Or will they persist in their course until they have the whole freshman class sitting on the floor playing with alphabet blocks?

Irwin Berger of Evander Childs High School, Bronx, New York, is an authority on audience reaction to language. In a series of eleven guide rules for semantic conciseness, he enhances Hayakawa's key concepts for communication success. Mr. Berger's second paper examines specific examples of student writing that are "fuzzy," confused, and invalid. Concerning the writing of relatively competent students, the author concludes, "Some readers may be so taken in by correct appearance that they may fail to notice the absence of good sense."

ELEVEN COMMON SENSE PRINCIPLES ABOUT LANGUAGE
and
STUDENT WRITING EXAMINED FOR LOGIC AND CLARITY

IRWIN BERGER*

Eleven Common Sense Principles about Language

1. *The word is not the thing.* You can't eat the word "apple" or shoot the word "gun." You can't get rid of Communists by removing the word "Communism" from textbooks.

Words are like maps. The more accurately the map describes the territory, the more useful it is. Maps can be wrong, and often are. There are outdated maps (beliefs and statements), make-believe "maps," deliberately misleading maps, well-intentioned but naive maps, maps that do not go into sufficient detail, maps that emphasize superhighways when you may be interested in winding country roads, etc.

2. *It's hard to pin down the meanings of general, abstract, relative terms.* Try to get beyond just words to the things they stand for. Know how reliable your sources of second- and third-hand information are. Before you write, examine the "territory" for yourself. Consider the facts with your own senses. Don't just rely on other people's *words*.

People misunderstand each other when they:

    a) use the same words while meaning different things, or

    b) use different words while meaning the same things.

Remember that practically all words, with the exception of some technical terms, have a number of different meanings. Don't just *hope* that your reader will get the particular meanings you intended; make yourself clear with specific examples.

For example, "Sure I said it was a *party*, but that doesn't mean there has to be dancing!" (The word "party" is a general term and means different things to different people.)

I lost my *blue crayon* (specific term), *clothing* (general), *freedom* (abstract), *appetite* (relative).

---

*Both articles are portions of Mr. Berger's dissertation, submitted February 1965, under supervision of Professor Solomon S. Simonson, to Yeshiva University, Graduate School of Education, Department of Language, Speech, and Communication (*Improving Composition through Emphasis on Semantics and Critical Thinking*). Used by permission of Irwin Berger and Yeshiva University.

3. *Context (not the dictionary) determines meaning.* *Bank* of snow . . . blood *bank* . . . *bank* on your support . . . dives from the *bank* . . . took money from the *bank* . . . *bank* the furnace . . . roads are *banked* on curves . . . where do you *bank* . . . *banks* of roses . . . a *bank* of swans . . . the jets *banked* in unison . . . we got stuck on the *bank* . . . you hold the *bank* . . . I'll be the *bank* . . . the *banks* of the organ . . . chained to the *banks* . . . etc.

King James referred to St. Paul's Cathedral as "amusing, awful, and artificial." He meant it as a compliment. In the eighteenth century, the words meant "amazing, awe-inspiring, and artistic."

Be especially cautious with pronouns. Any pronoun can contribute to vagueness and confusion unless you make perfectly clear what it refers to in the previous sentence or sentences.

—Charles told Captain Boyle that *he* had inherited a considerable sum of money from *his* cousin. Who? Whose cousin?

4. *Don't mix up inferences and facts.* When you talk about what you know "for a fact," or even what you have actually seen with your own eyes, how accurate are you? Would most people agree with what you say? Are you sure they would? Would you bet a dollar that you're right? A hundred dollars? Most people guess about things much more than they realize. Learn to distinguish inferences, assumptions, judgments, and opinions from facts.

a) REPORT: The poorly dressed man was slumped against the doorway.
   INFERENCE: The man is drunk. (What are the facts?)
b) REPORT: George was here the day the watch disappeared.
   INFERENCE: George took the watch. (What are the facts?)
c) REPORT: A doctor's car is parked in front of Mr. Smith's house.
   INFERENCE: Someone is sick. (What are the facts?)

A fact is a statement:
   a. that can be verified—
   b. by impersonal means—
   c. and applies to a particular person or situation at a particular time at a
      particular place.

Put mental quotation marks around the words "fact" and "true" to remind yourself how hard it is to be sure about anything.

Are the following statements "true" or "false"? (Apply the a-b-c formula above.)
   "It is raining."
   "He is an enemy."
   "This product will make you look younger, feel younger."

5. *There are different kinds of truth.*
   a) "This watermelon weighs 8½ pounds, and at 6 cents a pound, it will
      cost you 51 cents." (*True* if it can be verified.)
   b) "That was an entertaining movie." (*True* if we agree that it is.)
   c) "Crime does not pay." (*True* — for you — if you believe it.)
   d) "The sum of the interior angles of a triangle is 180 degrees." (*True* within
      an arbitrary system of geometry developed by Euclid.)

Many intellectual problems are questions of classification — that is, deciding what to call something. Is medicine a profession or a trade? Are tomatoes fruits or vegetables? Are farmers who operate oil wells on their land eligible for government "farm" benefits?

Such matters are decided by majority consent or by judges whose opinions we are willing to accept. The "truth" of such matters is arbitrary.

Many "truths" in matters of religion, ethics, esthetics, and philosophy cannot be verified by impersonal means and are therefore matters of faith, wishing, or belief. The "truth" of philosophical statements — if they cannot be expressed in concrete terms — can probably never be demonstrated by verifiable means.

It is fruitless for persons of conflicting beliefs to argue over the "truth" of what they are asserting — unless they make concrete statements which can then be subjected to verification.

In your writing, consider whether your assertions are facts, inferences, beliefs, wishes, hopes, or expressions of faith. It is foolish to be dogmatic about the first four because they can be checked out. It is not practical to argue about the last two.

6. *Some statements inform; others try to direct us. Beware of using the word "is" to make false equations and judgments.* Don't use the word "is" to plaster huge oversimplifying labels over people and things.

"Mr. Jones *is* a Republican." In your mind, you may register this statement as "Mr. Jones equals Republican." However, there is a lot more to Mr. Jones than the word "Republican" implies, even if the assertion is true. The verb "to be" followed by a predicate adjective or noun often expresses a matter of opinion rather than of fact:

—That joke was funny. Johnny is a delinquent. He is a coward. She is honest. Those curtains are green. This food is delicious. Snakes are delightful pets.

Beware of which of these statements inform and which try to direct us:

Lawrence Olivier plays Shakespearean roles. (INFORMS)
Lawrence Olivier is a great actor. (DIRECTS)
All men are mortal. (INFORMS)
All men are equal before the law. (DIRECTS)

Note that "is" has two safe, fundamental, and necessary uses:

1) as an auxiliary verb (e.g., She *is* dancing; we *are* ready; they have *been* sleeping.) There *is* informs.
2) as a verb of "being" (e.g., I *am* an American; Chicago *is* in Illinois; there *are* ten pills in the bottle) There *is* informs.

"Is" tends to be unsafe when we use it to project our own feelings (e.g., "Stamp collecting *is* a stupid hobby.") or when we use it as an "equal sign" of identity (e.g., "Johnny *is* a delinquent.") There *is* directs.

One way to avoid the pitfalls of the unsafe uses of "is" is to say what a person or thing *does* rather than what it *is*. Be concerned with what the purpose of something is rather than what you call it. It is easier for people to agree on descriptions of behavior or action than it is for them to agree on the significance or meaning of events. In view of these cautions, we will rewrite the examples in Topic 6:

"That joke was funny," becomes, "Everyone laughed at the joke."

"Johnny is a delinquent," becomes, "Johnny took a piece of chalk without permission."

"This is a wonderful automobile," becomes, "It hasn't had a breakdown in 50,000 miles."

"This is an amazing gadget," becomes, "This tool peels potatoes and scrapes carrots."

7. *Words have hidden emotional content.* When we express our personal feelings or prejudices, we like to think that what we say about a thing or person is actually true and that all the world sees it exactly as we do. But many descriptions reveal far more about the speaker than about what is described, e.g.:

—*Macbeth* is a stupid play.

—Dirty books like *Sister Carrie* and *The Grapes of Wrath* should be banned.

—There is no finer place to live than Cleveland, Ohio.

—Watching football on television is a great way to spend a Sunday afternoon in the fall.

Almost everyone uses a "stacked deck," "loaded words," when he talks or writes.

—I am firm; you are obstinate; he is pigheaded.

—We are careful with our money; they are very cheap.

—I am cautious; you are timid; they are cowardly.

—I am slender; you are rather thin; she is skinny.

Some statements express little more than whether a speaker or writer likes or dislikes something, whether he is for or against it — in short, whether he is *snarling* or *purring* at it:

—That's a brilliantly simple solution to a complex problem!

—That's much too obvious to work!

—She's lovely.

Note how "that mangy cur," "that lovable pup," "that silly pooch," "that vicious animal," may all refer to the same dog — depending on your emotional attitude toward it.

8. *Know that you are abstracting: control your generalizations.* Words tell only a little about the nature of things.

We do not realize how much abstracting we are doing all the time. We often select, without realizing why, some details of a situation while we fail to see or take proper notice of all the others. Arrogance, intolerance of others' viewpoints, frustration, and closed-mindedness are often the consequences.

—"I didn't get into Arista (or the college of my choice): I am a complete failure."

—"Now that we have put Telstar into orbit, television will be able to wipe out illiteracy in Africa and Asia."

Avoid looking for *the* answer to a problem. Use plurals. Deal with problems, causes, questions, solutions, interpretations, etc.

—"The reason I am having trouble with Miss Thompson is . . ."

—"The cause of last week's stock market rise . . ."

Surely, there must be more than one "reason," more than one "cause."

A simple device to help you to avoid overgeneralizing is to add "etc." to your statements and descriptions. (But be sure you understand what "etc." means; it should not be used, for example, as a substitute for thinking up concrete examples.)

Avoid sweeping generalizations: "Men are all alike." "Women are poor drivers." "Good athletes make poor students." "I'm going to prove that the United States is ahead of Russia in the race for space."

9. *The disease of "Allness" and "Either-or" thinking.* "Allness" occurs when you unconsciously assume that you know or have already said *everything* that is important about something. Stop trying to simplify complex issues and processes. Neither should you go to the other extreme and give too much weight to relatively minor occurrences.

Some people see the world in black and white terms. They fail to see the shades of color. Avoid "either-or" thinking. Use the "How Much?" index, the habit of asking "how much?" or "to what degree?" something is so. Girls are not beautiful *or* dumb. Boys are not *either* brawny *or* brainy. People are not *either* entirely honest *or* entirely dishonest; a person is not *either* a success *or* a failure; happy *or* miserable.

—"You're either a friend or an enemy, with us or against us!"

—"There are two sides to every question."

Not so! There may be many sides to a question.

In a divorce, who is at fault — he or she? Probably both, *to a degree.* Avoid the childlike and artificial oversimplifications of popular music ("All, or nothing at all . . .") and of cheap fiction in which people are either good or bad.

Try these correctives for "allness":

a) Consider whether there are *only* two possibilities. ("This bill must be passed to prevent our way of life from being destroyed.")

b) Specify the degree, tell "how much" something is so. Be specific. ("The boy was tall, 5′ 11″, for his age, 13.")

c) Activate your vocabulary. For example, what do you mean specifically when you say: "It's a nice day; we had a terrible time; it's a nice song; he said terrible things about you; she wore a terrible dress last night." There are several hundred adjectives available to substitute for "nice" or "terrible."

d) Qualify your statements with such terms as: *very, moderately, slightly, extremely, generally, seldom, probably, possibly, tends to,* etc.

By themselves, these terms won't insure accuracy in your writing, but they *may* help.

—"Teenagers prefer popular to classical and folk music." (Add "Some," "Many," or even "Most" and see how much less "either-or-ish" the sentence becomes.)

"Never" write that *all* Americans are this or that . . .; "never" write that something *always* or *never* happens. You might even have difficulty proving that "*Most* people believe that . . ."

You put yourself out on a shaky limb when you claim to know (or that anyone knows) *all* about anything.

10. *Time means change. Use the "When" Index.* Maybe photographs don't change, but people do. Avoid the childish habit of unconsciously believing that the way you see a person, process, object, or situation *now* is the way it has always been and will always be. Everything changes — all the time.

Even "facts" change. Before 1930, when the planet Pluto was discovered, there "were" only eight planets in our solar system. There *may* be ten or more in the future. (Be sure to check the dates of publication of your reference books.)

Use the "When" Index. Put dates on your snapshots so that you can keep them in order and in proper perspective.

—Mary Jones (senior in high school, June 1962) is not the "same" person as Mary Jones (freshman, September 1958).

—John Kennedy (1962: President) was not John Kennedy (1955: Senator) was not John Kennedy (1935: Teenager).

Once a word is spoken or written down, it remains fixed even though the thing, person, or event it describes continues to develop and change.

11. *Identity: No two things are ever the same.* Things may be similar, but they are never identical. Language encourages us to categorize and classify our experiences. People tend to emphasize similarities and to minimize or ignore differences. We often lump things together, but White Pill (1) is not White Pill (2); Blue, Four-Door 1961 Chevrolet Sedan (1) is not Blue, Four-Door 1961 Chevrolet Sedan (2); Negro (1) is not Negro (2); etc.

An important aspect of common sense is the ability to see the differences between things that are superficially alike.

Some Aids to More Thoughtful Compositions

1. *Etc.*   A device to indicate that you are aware that you cannot say all (or know all) about anything.

2. *Indexing*   A device to indicate that no two things are identical, that no word has exactly the same meaning twice. Examples: Democracy (USA) is not Democracy (USSR); Teenager in Dungarees (1) is not Teenager in Dungarees (2).

3. *Dating*   A device to indicate that no thing is ever twice the same. (Refer to Topic 10. Use the "When" Index: Mary (1955) is not Mary (1962); Elevator (this morning) is not Elevator (this afternoon).

4. *Quotes*   A device to indicate that a word is not being used in its usual sense; sometimes a kind of shorthand for "so-called." Example: Even "facts" can change.

5. It is awkward and unnecessary to write out these devices except, at times, for emphasis. The place to apply them is inside your head.

6. Avoid saying *all, always, never, completely,* etc., about anything. Include details and exceptions.

7. Use the "Roller Coaster" method for writing better essays. Alternate, in a general way, between abstract and concrete thoughts, between generalizations and specific illustrations and "proofs."

Every time you write *for example* on an essay examination and give a pertinent illustration, you are probably gaining points toward a higher grade.

Paragraphs in examination essays and compositions, which are predominately abstract, philosophical, or theoretical tend to be weak. Paragraphs which are merely an accumulation of specific facts and details without conclusions or generalizations drawn from them tend to be weak. Use the Roller Coaster method: mix general and specific, abstract and concrete thoughts alternate frequently from one to the other.

Apply the same principle — of variety — to the length of your sentences. Do not write consistently in very long or very short sentences. Be sparing with long sentences (e.g., those with more than twenty words). In general, long sentences are harder to read than medium and short length sentences.

8. Etc.

Summary of Common Sense Language Habits

A Naive Writer:	A Sophisticated Writer:
Uses absolute terms, allness terms, abstractions without illustrations	Uses descriptive terms, gives specific data, illustrations, etc.
Uses emotionally loaded words	Uses neutral terms, speaks in terms of "more or less," degrees, and shades of meaning
Uses "either-or" arguments, speaks *positively* "for" or "against"	
Confuses facts, inferences, judgments	Distinguishes facts, inferences, and judgments
Labels situations, people, problems	Differentiates among situations, people, and problems
Is tradition-oriented, relies on "authority" and second- and third-hand information	Has an open-minded attitude, refers to facts, experiments, tries to make his own evaluations, etc.
Etc.	Etc.

Six Reminders for Sophisticated Language Use

Attach these (mentally or actually) to your statements and assertions.

1. *As Far As I Know:* A reminder that it is impossible to be absolutely certain about anything. Consider the following assertions:
  —The plane crashed because of faulty wiring in the tail section (as far as I know). There may be reasons I know nothing about.
  —He succeeded in business because he followed my advice.
  —This gun is not loaded.
  —He is an honest man (as far as I know).
  —That dog does not bite.
  —There can be no life on the moon because there is no water there.

2. *To a Point:* A reminder that things are "true" in varying degrees and "to a certain extent" only.
  —This plant doesn't need much light to grow. ("True" to a point.)
  —This paper is white.
  —This is a valuable coin.

—This coat is worn out.

—I will lend you some money if you need it.

—The weather report says that it won't rain tomorrow.

—He doesn't like you because you forget his birthday.

—The plane crashed because of faulty wiring in the tail section.

3. *To Me (in My Opinion):* A reminder that each person *reacts* in his own particular way; a reminder that people react differently to the same things.

—This soup is too salty (for me).

—The radio isn't being played loud enough (for me).

—That's a very funny story (to me).

—The stock market crashed because we have a Democratic (or Republican) President (in my opinion).

—The plane crashed because of faulty wiring in the tail section.

Many statements convey more information about the feelings of the speaker or writer than they do about the objects referred to:

When a high school pupil writes, "*Macbeth* is a lousy play," he is revealing more about himself than the play.

The statement "William Alexander Smith is a great man!" merely tells us the writer's *opinion* but not much about Smith.

When your friend says, "She's the *sweetest, kindest,* most *beautiful* girl in the world," he may be looking through love-colored glasses.

(Note: The first three topics are general reminders that the answers to most questions are multiple and complex and that we are bound to overlook some important details and underlying causes of anything we are trying to explain.)

4. *The What Index:* A reminder that no two things or situations are ever exactly alike in *all* respects. Interview (1) is not interview (2). History teacher (1) is not history teacher (2). Twenty-dollar bill (1) is not twenty-dollar bill (2) or (3).

5. *The When Index:* A reminder that all things *change.* Weather (today) is different from weather (tonight). Your mood (8 a.m.) is not your mood (8 p.m.)

Your first or early impressions of people, places, and things tend to stick firmly in your mind and remain unchanged. It takes effort and common sense to keep your impressions revised and up to date.

6. *The Where Index:* A reminder that persons and things change depending on where they happen to be at the time.

—Flower (on a bush) is different from flower (in a vase).

—Flower (in a vase with water) is different from flower (in a vase without water).

(Note: The *What, When,* and *Where Indexes* are general reminders to pay attention to important *differences* in identity, time, and place.)

The more we examine language habits, the more we see that language is an abstracting process, and that the way we write about things tends to be highly selective, arbitrary, and distorting:

Highly selective: We leave out far more than we express;

Arbitrary: What we put in or leave out isn't always logical or clear to the reader (or even to the writer);

Distorting: Even what we consciously choose to say, we may say incorrectly or confusingly.

The everyday language habits which you have been practicing all your life have become so natural with you that even if you were to memorize the preceding principles and reminders and determine to use them correctly, you would still continue to make many of the old mistakes.

It is no simple matter to develop a sophisticated awareness of words. But the dividends, in more effective speaking and writing, make the effort very much worthwhile.

Student Writing Examined for Logic and Clarity

If it didn't take special effort, more pupils would probably write their compositions with logic and clarity. But teachers, editors, and employers have much difficulty persuading some pupils to put in the extra effort to attain these two qualities.

Following are some examples of poor writing with suggestions on how to improve them. The selections are worth studying. A variety of weaknesses are discussed, some minor, some major. The objective is not to correct one or two particular types of errors *but the general attitude of indifference to precision and coherence.*

Example 1:

"Morte D'Arthur" by Sir Thomas Malory is considered the best English prose of its century.

This is a correct and intelligent sentence, but there are two weaknesses. The pupil fails to mention what century *Morte D'Arthur* comes from. And the verb, *is considered,* begs the question: "Who considers it the best—the pupil, his teachers, the general public?" A more careful writer might have written:

"Morte D'Arthur" by Sir Thomas Malory is generally considered by critics and historians to be the best English prose of the fifteenth century.

or . . .

In survey texts of English literature (or In "Adventures in English Literature" by Inglis and Spear) Sir Thomas Malory's "Morte D'Arthur" is called the best English prose of the fifteenth century.

There's little point in saying that the pupil might have added (or did add) the missing information "in the next sentence, or paragraph." He has missed the opportunity for clarity and completeness in *this* sentence.

The differences between the original and the corrected sentences are greater than most pupils care to admit. They will agree grudgingly that the corrected versions are more complete and probably more effective, but they "don't know what the big fuss is all about." The big fuss concerns the degree to which a student (reporter, writer, employee) is willing to deal with the responsibilities of written communication.

Example 2:

> *Whenever American railroaders tell of daring deeds, they mention Casey Jones.*

The pupil should realize that it is very unlikely that he can make such an assertion with any certainty. In fact, he can probably bet on the fact that some American railroaders have never heard of Casey Jones. The sentence is more "reasonable" rewritten as follows:

> *The daring deeds of Casey Jones stand out in the legendary history of American railroads.* (Or the like.)

Example 3:

> *I will prove in this essay that the United States is either tied with Russia or ahead of Russia in the space field.*

Needless to say, the 300 words that followed this topic sentence (however patriotic) *proved* very little except that some pupils are naive about the complexities of world events, and unaware of the rigors of substantiating their beliefs, hopes, and desires with cold facts.

In elementary school and even in junior and senior high school, pupils are given much encouragement to be fancy free in their writing. In academic high school courses, however, and almost without exception in college, written work is expository and analytical. Many pupils find it hard to make the transition from off the cuff to responsible writing.

Example 4:

> *The Chinese Nationalists occupying Formosa were forced there as a last resort when the Communists invaded China about twenty years ago.*

When the teacher questioned the pupil about the word *invaded*, the pupil explained that she had meant *revolution*. She knew the difference all along but was not much bothered by her essay-writing conscience for using a "similar" (but strikingly incorrect) word. You just cannot get by on examinations and in college with words that are approximately what you mean.

Another criticism of the same sentence is that the expression *as a last resort* is uselessly vague and must be explained if it is to earn any credit in an essay test.

Example 5:

> *The future of the free world depends entirely on whether we are strong enough to remain permanently "the" world power. Therefore, without the proper training of America's youth, we will be destined to change our economic and social system. However, I believe we will not be left in the dust by Russia, and that in the very near future we will again lead the world in every conceivable manner.*

The chief weakness of this example is not that it is "incorrect" but that it is vague and thoughtless. The pupil uses many terms which have fuzzy boundaries of meaning.

The future of the free world . . . . Does he mean the immediate future, next month, the next 100 years? What is *the free world?* Are Egypt, Yugoslavia, and the Union of South Africa included?

. . . depends entirely on whether we are strong enough to remain permanently "the" *world power . . . . What,* precisely, depends on *what?* What will Russia be doing while we *. . . remain permanently* (?) *"the" world power?* How strong is *strong enough?*

. . . therefore (therefore—what?) *without the proper training of America's youth . . .* (It would take more than one composition to explain what *proper training* is.) *. . . we will be destined* (?) *to change our economic and social system* (from what to what?).

. . . However, I believe . . . (for what reasons beside hope?) *we will not be left in the dust . . .* (Explain.) *by Russia, and that in the very near future . . .* (Next week, month?) *we will again lead . . .* (*Again?* When did we stop leading?) *the world in every conceivable manner. . . .* (*Every?* Can't we allow Russia the satisfaction of excelling us in *anything?*)

Despite the fact that the example contains no errors in written English, it is too meaningless to earn many points in a school essay. The topic is too complex, too broad to be treated in such thoughtless clichés and unsubstantiated generalizations.

By the time a pupil is a high school senior or a college freshman, it is time for him to come to grips intelligently with so *important* a topic.

Example 6:

> *President Lincoln was confronted with many serious problems, and when war broke out, his party began to doubt his ability. But his intellect and determination proved him capable of handling the situation.*

If these are *topic sentences* (that is, introductory sentences) and if the pupil follows them up with a paragraph of specific illustrations and references — he will probably earn a high mark in a social studies essay test. But as so frequently happens, a pupil writes a few reasonably good *general* sentences like these, and then stops — or goes on to another topic and *more* broad, general sentences. Whenever you make a general statement such as *was confronted with serious problems,* you have an obligation to prove your point with specific examples.

Example 7:

> *Sherlock Holmes, with his associate, Dr. Watson, solved some of the most difficult cases in the history of fiction. Today's police would do well to follow some of his methods of crime detection.*

Here is an excellent example of the kind of essay writing that many bright students hand in to their teachers. As you can see, the two sentences are free from mechanical errors, they are smoothly written, and they "sound intelligent." However, they are counterfeit!

Unless he is prepared to give at least two detailed illustrations of Holmes' "methods," and show, also, that present day detectives do *not* use them, the pupil has merely climbed out on a long limb. The more you consider these two sentences, the more obvious it becomes that they are thoughtless, invalid, and "insincere." It is most unlikely that the pupil knows enough about modern crime detection to state with any certainty that Sherlock Holmes used methods which today's detectives neglect or fail to use.

What is good preparation for written composition work in college? What plans are being tried for more effectively articulating high school and college teaching of writing? This article deals with these questions on a national basis. Dr. Grommon is a professor of English and education at Stanford University and edited the NCTE volume on The Education of Teachers of English.

COORDINATING COMPOSITION IN HIGH SCHOOL AND COLLEGE*

Alfred H. Grommon

Defining Good Writing

Most teachers of secondary school English probably do not have a chance to find out directly what the colleges mean specifically when they say that students must be able to write a "passing essay." Even investigating the nature of college freshman English courses may not help teachers much because these courses differ so much throughout the country. However great these differences may be, though, the core of each of them still seems to be the writing of a "passing expository essay." The grades in a great many courses are determined almost exclusively by the instructors' evaluation of the written compositions. High school teachers of college preparatory students should especially note that freshmen are required to write expository essays based largely upon their readings. Some essays, however, are explanations of how something works or is done, or are extended definitions, or presentations of evidence to support a conviction or a side of an argument. So the high school teachers preparing students for college should assign themes that require students to think about impersonal matters rather than those that entice them merely to recount personal experience or to uncork emotions.

I have borrowed from the College Entrance Examination Board's 1958 *Advanced Placement Program Syllabus* (page 95) the best statement I have seen of the kinds of skills in thinking and writing that colleges dream of their students having. These criteria are used to judge whether the high school seniors taking the Advanced Placement Examination in Literature and Composition can think and write as college freshmen are expected to:

> Advanced work in composition teaches students to write well about something important. The core of training in composition is therefore the frequent writing and careful revision of substantial themes on subjects sufficiently mature to challenge both thought and linguistic powers. These themes should be distinguished by superior command of *substance*, thoughtfully and interestingly presented.
>
> A good student writer will demonstrate a high level of proficiency in *organization*, combining clear sentences in well-shaped paragraphs and arranging these in an order clear to the reader as well as to himself. He is well aware of the importance of organic structure, distinguishes the major parts and the subdivisions of the whole, and deliberately develops his paper with a sense

---

*From Alfred H. Grommon, "Coordinating Composition in High School and College," *English Journal*, XLVIII (March 1959), 123-131. Used by permission of Alfred H. Grommon.

of controlling purpose and orderly progression.

However, a neat pattern of paragraphs is not in itself proof of, and can never be an acceptable substitute for, sound and compelling logic. The good student writer will be sufficiently an analyst of his own ideas to avoid *non sequiturs* and redundancies. He is careful to support general statements with specific proofs; he distinguishes between causes and effects, between subjective reactions and objective judgments; and he has cultivated the ability to select fresh rather than hackneyed illustrations.

A good composition exhibits a feeling for style, displaying both *precision* and *fluency*. An able student will make use of the varieties of English sentence structure. His sensitivity to sentence movement will be heightened by exposure to good models; a strong student, however, will have absorbed such influences well enough so that his style remains his own. His vocabulary will be distinguished not so much by its extent as by its exactness and appropriateness.

It should go without saying that a student in an advanced course will have mastered the *mechanics* of writing. His command of the conventions of spelling, capitalization, and punctuation will be firm; his syntax will be clear and accurate.

Teachers who are looking for a guide to help them plan a writing program that will correlate closely with what the colleges expect might well develop the above statement — sentence by sentence — into a step-by-step process of teaching students how to think and how to compose a composition.

Although teachers of Advanced Placement courses may assume perhaps that their students have "mastered" the conventions of punctuation, capitalization, usage, spelling, and syntax, I judge that most teachers cannot afford the luxury of this assumption and hence would like more specific guidance on how they should teach their students to use these conventions appropriately. For guidance on this aspect of writing, teachers should consult David M. Litsey's valuable report of his analysis of the content of the objective English placement tests used by 142 colleges in forty-four states and the District of Columbia. His article, "Trends in College Placement Tests in Freshman English," was published in the *English Journal* of May 1956. Mr. Litsey's findings not only identify the kinds of evidence the colleges are seeking but also annihilate many teachers' misconceptions of these tests and thereby destroy the fictitious props that some teachers have used to shore up shaky programs of teaching erroneous notions of English grammar, usage, and syntax and of ways of teaching writing. Mr. Litsey concludes that:

> In the final analysis, therefore, it may be stated confidently that colleges no longer are interested in whether an entering student knows technical grammatical terminology, punctuation rules, evanescent pronunciations, or the like, but rather colleges are concerned with proof that a student can actually use language to good effect.

Critical Thinking Vital

It seems to me that in saying colleges want proof a student can "use language to good effect" Mr. Litsey is implying also what is clearly specified about "compelling logic" in the third paragraph of the quotation from the *Advanced Place-*

ment Program Syllabus. The indispensable prelude to using language to good effect and to the logic of all worthwhile communication is thinking. Today, it is hard to find a statement of the purposes of education in the United States that does not stress the importance of teaching all students how to think. Statements of this purpose appear in many of the NCTE's publications and in many of the courses of study developed in the schools and colleges. Yet, in my study of these materials, I seldom find any detailed suggestions of how we should teach students to think. Even more rarely do I find any indication that teachers of English are at all aware of their unsurpassed opportunities to teach students to think.

The kind of thinking I have in mind is suggested in the preceding quotation from the *APP Syllabus.* It is the kind of reflective thinking defined by John Dewey as being "Active, persistent, and careful consideration of any belief or supposed form of knowledge in the light of the grounds that support it, and the further conclusions to which it tends . . ."[1] It is what is commonly called "critical think ing," not critical in the sense of being carping, adverse, cynical, negative, destruc tive, but in the sense of being judicious.

We know from research not only that the attitudes and skills that constitute critical thinking *can* be taught but also that they *must* be taught to many students *directly.* Although some people apparently develop these attitudes and skills independently, we teachers cannot assume that our students will somehow, on their own, learn to think logically, to distinguish fact from opinion, to support generalizations with valid evidence, and to avoid common fallacies in reasoning. We must directly help our students acquire these awarenesses and skills.

I believe that in teaching students to compose compositions and in *evaluating* their papers, teachers in the elementary and secondary schools and colleges have both an inescapable responsibility and made-to-order opportunities to teach students to think critically. I am afraid, however, that colleges' and schools' efforts to improve students' preparation for college, particularly for college English, have been so concentrated upon the more obvious matters of merely proofread- ing papers — the kind of clerical job any bright student in class can probably do just as well — that we seem to have failed to look at the papers as indelible demonstrations of how students think and of the values by which they live and judge.

Although I do not have time here to develop in detail this important aspect of teaching thinking and writing in the schools and colleges, I would like to offer a few suggestions. One important step is to try to convert as many as possible of our writing assignments into problems to be worked upon and, whenever feasible, some conclusions reached. I think that the more successful we are in selecting and phrasing problems that are meaningful to our students, the better are our chances of maneuvering students into doing some thinking about what they have to say on these issues. We should capitalize upon issues that arise in class, in school, or in the community that will get the students involved in mar- shalling evidence and in trying to work out reasoned solutions. Once enmeshed

---

[1]John Dewey, *How We Think* (Boston: D. C. Heath and Co., 1910), p. 6.

in a problem with which they are genuinely concerned, they may also find themselves, almost unbeknownst to them, trying to compose a decent presentation
of their arguments and proposals. Such motivation is invaluable.

For college preparatory students, these essays and problems should be largely
related to the literature they are reading. Such assignments are almost univer-
sally used in college freshman English courses. Joseph Mersand, in his guides to
Sunrise at Campobello and *West Side Story*, has provided some excellent examples of suitable topics for guiding students to an understanding of what is at
work in these selections and for problem-solving themes.[2] Here are three:

1. The French critic Brunetière said that a drama was a "conflict of will."
   Show several instances of the conflict of wills in *Sunrise at Campobello*.
2. What would you call the underlying meaning of *Sunrise at Campobello* in
   terms of human values? Can you recall other plays or novels in which this
   same underlying meaning (or idea) is found? How does this theme make
   more meaningful F.D.R.'s political and human accomplishments?
3. The song, "Gee, Officer Krupke," has been a controversial one in the play
   (*West Side Story*). On the one hand it has been called "the most hilarious
   travesty of our times" by John McClain, reviewer of the New York *Journal-
   American*. Harold Clurman, writing in *The Nation*, called it a comic parody
   which made him resentful. Discuss the relevance of both arguments. Is it
   defensible as an example of comic relief? Should such a topic as the treatment of juvenile delinquency be treated in such fashion?

This type of assignment for compositions requires students to use problem-solving
methods and the other attitudes and skills of critical thinking.

In the course of our teaching them to select, organize, and present materials
for such assignments, and – of equal importance – in our evaluations of their
thinking exhibited in their discussions and compositions, we should be teaching
them some of the following attitudes and skills:

I. *Techniques of problem solving*
    A. Recognizing and defining problems
    B. Considering hypotheses
    C. Evaluating the nature and relevance of evidence
    D. Organizing evidence appropriately
    E. Relating conclusions to evidence
    F. Distinguishing hypotheses from assumptions and conclusions
    G. Qualifying conclusions
    H. Testing conclusions
    I. Avoiding misapplication of conclusions
    J. Altering conclusions if necessary in the light of testing

II. *Assumptions and definitions*
    A. Recognizing assumptions and trying to avoid using too many of them
    B. Defining terms, but trying to avoid faulty definitions

---

[2]*Drama Studies*, I (February 1958 and August 1958, respectively) (Summit, New Jersey:
Educational and Recreational Guides, Inc.)

     C. Avoiding shifts in meaning of terms without warning or without the
        writer's or speaker's recognizing the shift

     D. Realizing the variety and shades of meanings a word may have in context

     E. Recognizing the distinctions between words and their referents

III. *Moral and spiritual values:* "In spite of relapses and variations in practice,
there is a generally accepted body of values which the American people
tend to use as a compass for finding their way through political, social,
economic, and personal issues."[3]

     A. Human personality — the basic value

     B. Moral responsibility

     C. Institutions as the servants of men

     D. Common consent

     E. Devotion to truth

     F. Respect for excellence

     G. Moral equality

     H. Brotherhood

     I. The pursuit of happiness

     J. Spiritual enrichment

IV. *Nature and use of evidence*

     A. Testing validity and appropriateness of evidence

     B. Providing adequate evidence

     C. Supporting assertions

     D. Noting qualifications of authority or source

     E. Being aware of the importance of evidence used or omitted

     F. Noting the relationship between supporting evidence and the purpose of
        its being used

V. *Generalizations*

     A. Generalizing from enough instances

     B. Avoiding and being aware of oversimplification

     C. Qualifying generalizations appropriately

     D. Avoiding and being aware of the use of stereotypes

VI. *Fallacies in reasoning to be avoided but recognized*

     A. *Non sequiturs*

     B. Attacking motives instead of arguments

     C. Arguing in a circle

     D. *Post hoc, ergo propter hoc*

     E. False analogy

     F. Appealing to emotions through using such devices as bandwagon, name
        calling, glittering generalities

    I conclude, then, with this recommendation. When college and high school
teachers of English work together to improve the articulation of the English programs to prepare students for college — and what is even more important, for

---

[3]Educational Policies Commission, National Education Association, *Moral and Spiritual
Values in the Public Schools* (Washington, D.C., 1951), pp. 17-30.

life — they should focus their attention also upon the ways in which teachers of English can help students to think effectively. Instead, for example, of looking upon the writing students do in high schools and college mainly as a showcase in which they display merely their ability to punctuate, spell, and capitalize, we must realize that in looking at the finished papers we are looking at much more: we are looking in upon the very ways in which students' minds work and upon the values by which they judge life as they experience it.

THE EVALUATOR: Which Standards Does He Meet, and How, with Large Paper Loads?

> "Joint Statement on Freshman English in College and High School Preparation" by the Departments of English of Ball State University, Indiana State College, Indiana University, and Purdue University
> "Marking the Paper" by Lou L. LaBrant
> "In Praise of Praise" by Paul B. Diederich
> "Managing Student Writing" by Sarah I. Roody
> "Some Semantic Implications of Theme Correction" by William J. Dusel
> "From Guided Theme Reading to Improved Writing" by Isidore Levine
> "A Magic Lantern for English" by Edwin L. Peterson

These seven essays deal with the problem of theme correction as related to college preparatory demands with emphasis on the positive approach. Authors of the "Joint Statement" clarify college writing requirements and define standards necessary for meeting them. Lou LaBrant applies these standards from a psychological viewpoint centering on the question, "Will your comments lead the student to write again or to fear writing?" Sarah Roody believes that involving the students themselves in the business of managing many papers and evaluating them with teacher guidance and direction is the answer to the problem.

William Dusel's observations, tallied from studies submitted by approximately 400 English teachers in California schools, center on the fact that students are confused, rather than enlightened, by the ambiguities of conventional symbols used in marking. He feels that "discouragement — resulting from the overmarked papers — begins in the lower grades." Mr. Dusel offers practical help away from "finding fault actively" and "enjoying passively." Paul B. Diederich suggests that teachers concentrate on one error at a time. He does not believe that "drowning errors in red ink" will help to improve student writing.

Isidore Levine maintains that early training in the art of theme reading by the students will alert them to the meaning and application of rules, to understanding of organization, and to the absolute need for clarity and logic of expression. He demonstrates his thesis by concrete examples. Edwin Peterson shares his experiment in the use of visual aids both in correcting and revising college freshman themes. The overhead projector is Mr. Peterson's answer to the need for instructing in large groups where individual help is not always available.

The "Joint Statement" was drawn up by the four colleges following a combined assessment of their first year English classes. It expresses in effect what has recently become cause for universal concern — the number of entering freshmen who are almost totally unequipped to read with any degree of understanding or to write with a semblance of efficiency. The statement's purpose, however, is clearly a positive one: to "recommend policies and practices" which may act as norms of competence for teachers of English at every level.

The sample student theme placed at the statement's opening may well have been titled, "Why Colleges Are Alarmed." The closing one, in contrast, demonstrates the hope that freshmen can be taught to write with competence and effectiveness.

JOINT STATEMENT ON FRESHMAN ENGLISH IN COLLEGE AND HIGH SCHOOL PREPARATION*

DEPARTMENTS OF ENGLISH (Indiana Colleges)

"MY PRINCIPAL DIFFICULTIES IN WRITING PAPER."

I have real rough time write paper in school today. It starts back in grade school about 1943 in Indianapolis, Indiana, I was in the forth grade in that year, My teach I remember was so nice to me, because I would ask her for help in English, the anwers was No—now to day. When passed time come, I missed —passed, because of this one thing. In the year to fellow My mother knew a old retire teacher, that was teacher when she was a girls, I ask her for help and was whole brand new life for me. When starts in the ninth grade in high school, theme were hard to write because I did now how to write complets sentence, noun, verb, pronoun, conjunction and many other things that happy to me. I was just on the side on grade time, my buy mark was in English one, I made a B. For next two and half year I made C. I think I should reserve those grade, should been lows. I do'not like to write theme at all, If I could learn to write theme, I think that I have compass a great deal. That is why I am at Indiana, U. this semester to take W 101 in English. If I can learn to write at Indiana U. I will gone on thought school and graduate. I think this plan that school is a very good one, to help out studant like me.

Too many students entering the four state colleges and universities cannot read with understanding or write clearly. So serious is the problem presented by increasing numbers of poorly trained college freshmen that we — the departments of English of Ball State Teachers College, Indiana State Teachers College, Indiana University, and Purdue University — have combined to issue this statement.

---

*Prepared by Departments of English of Ball State University, Indiana State College, Indiana University, and Purdue University, published by cooperating institutions, pp. 1-4, 17-19. Used by permission of Donald J. Gray.

Our purpose is not to criticize the teachers of English in elementary and secondary schools — who are not, of course, solely responsible for the weakness of their students in the use of language — or to impose a pattern of teaching on them. Our purpose, rather, is to clarify college requirements, and to recommend policies and practices that we believe will help English teachers at all levels in our mutual task of guiding students towards a necessary competence in reading and writing.

In preparing this statement, we have agreed as to what abilities in English entering college freshmen should have. We have agreed on standards by which their writing will be measured in our four institutions. We have considered what elementary and high school teachers of English can do — with help from other teachers and from the community — to prepare their students for successful work in college. We have affirmed our conviction that English should be taught only by properly qualified persons unburdened by excessive teaching loads and extracurricular duties.[1] And we are publishing the following policies and recommendations so that the widest possible attention can be given them by teachers, school administrators, and the public generally.

I. Required Abilities in English for Students Entering College

A. WRITING: We expect an entering student to write well enough

> to present his ideas in logical and clearly constructed sentences and paragraphs;
> to develop these into an organized unit;
> to be free from fear that mechanical errors may distort or cloud his meaning;
> to be confident that his ideas will be understood and respected.

In college he will increase his competence as he writes on more mature and more difficult subjects.

B. READING: We expect an entering student to read adult prose and poetry well enough

> to gain from his reading accurate information and ideas;
> to interpret these in terms of his own experience;
> to recognize their organization;
> to analyze and evaluate them.

In college he will increase these abilities as he reads more mature, provocative, and difficult material.

We strongly urge greater classroom attention to masterpieces of English and American literature as a means of acquainting high school students with our rich literary and cultural heritage, of improving their ability to read critically, and of developing their ability to write well.

II. Grading Standards in Freshman Composition

We have agreed upon uniform standards in the grading of student papers in

---

[1] We call the attention of administrators and the public to two recent studies: "Teaching Load of Teachers of English in Indiana," *Bulletin of the School of Education, Indiana University*, Volume 32 (May 1956); and James B. Conant, *The American High School Today* (New York, 1959), pp. 50-51.

our freshman composition programs. We feel that knowledge of these grading standards will be useful to high school teachers in preparing their students for college.

Each paper written in a freshman composition course — class theme, outside essay, term paper — is evaluated on the basis of five criteria: *content, organization, sentence structure, diction,* and *mechanics* (grammar, spelling, and punctuation). The table on page 26 describes these criteria.

The following is an application of our recommended procedures and practices. The theme was written for a college freshman English class.

Saturday Invaders

Wordy and weak

[There is quite an assortment] of Saturday students found within a music school in a metropolitan area. Within the ivy-covered walls during the week, all is quiet as can be expected in a music school. Nearly all of the college students are students in every sense of

Punct.

the word. But on Saturdays pandemonium breaks loose with the invasion by "students" between the ages of five and eighteen.

There are very young children whose doting parents are aspiring for them to attain the heights of musical achievement. These children may be separated into two groups. There are those who are what their parents have hoped; there are also those who would rather be anywhere in the world but at a music school. To them, music is a *Ref. Do these pronouns refer to the first, to the second, or to both groups?* thing to be unhappily endured. They are easily distinguished from one another at orchestra rehearsal. The first group listens with rapt attention to the conductor's instructions and explanations. With swinging feet that can't quite reach the floor, the others let their eyes wander over the faces of the people who are listening to *Find another word. You have already used "group"* the rehearsal. The heads of these erstwhile young musicians move as though on pivots, much to the consternation of the harassed conductor.

Repetitious and monotonous structure.

The high school students constitute the next large age group. *to describe varieties of* There are, of course, a few near-geniuses, but very few. Most of them *students of the same age.* come stumbling through the corridor and up the stairs with only the

	CONTENT	ORGANIZATION: Rhetorical and Logical Development	ORGANIZATION: Sentence Structure	DICTION	GRAMMAR, PUNCTUATION, SPELLING
Superior (A-B)	A significant central idea clearly defined, and supported with concrete, substantial, and consistently relevant detail	Theme planned so that it progresses by clearly ordered and necessary stages, and developed with originality and consistent attention to proportion and emphasis; paragraphs coherent, unified, and effectively developed; transitions between paragraphs explicit and effective	Sentences skilfully constructed (unified, coherent, forceful, effectively varied)	Distinctive: fresh, precise, economical, and idiomatic	Clarity and effectiveness of expression promoted by consistent use of standard grammar, punctuation, and spelling
Average (C)	Central idea apparent but trivial, or trite, or too general; supported with concrete detail, but detail that is occasionally repetitious, irrelevant, or sketchy	Plan and method of theme apparent but not consistently fulfilled; developed with only occasional disproportion or inappropriate emphasis; paragraphs unified, coherent, usually effective in their development; transitions between paragraphs clear but abrupt, mechanical, or monotonous	Sentences correctly constructed but lacking distinction	Appropriate: clear and idiomatic	Clarity and effectiveness of expression weakened by occasional deviations from standard grammar, punctuation, and spelling
Unacceptable (D-F)	Central idea lacking, or confused, or unsupported with concrete and relevant detail	Plan and purpose of theme not apparent; undeveloped or developed with irrelevance, redundancy, or inconsistency; paragraphs incoherent, not unified, or undeveloped; transitions between paragraphs unclear or ineffective	Sentences not unified, incoherent, fused, incomplete, monotonous, or childish	Inappropriate: vague, unidiomatic, or substandard	Communication obscured by frequent deviations from standard grammar, punctuation, and spelling

Logic? Are they able to keep up the conversation because they haven't practiced?

score of last night's game fresh in their minds. [Since they haven't had much time to practice during the week,] and since even music teachers sometimes like to hear a play-by-play account of the latest basketball game, these team-happy musicians often manage to keep a rather one-sided conversation going for twenty-five minutes of their half-hour lesson periods. A full day of teaching of this type pro-vides an unscheduled rest for these teachers.

Ambiguous: this type of teaching or this type of student?

   Some of the high school music students play in the student orchestra also, sitting unashamedly beside and between some of the little geniuses. [This is another basis for consternation on the con-ductor's part.] How can he ever have an orchestra that looks balanced in size when a minute boy of nine years plays first chair cornet while a lanky high school senior plays second? As soon as a break in the rehearsal is declared, there is a unanimous stampede in the direction of the ice cream machine. This is the only time when it's impossible to distinguish the geniuses from the ordinary people.

Wordy

   Finally, Saturday draws to an end, and as the invaders begin to leave, the regular students begin to emerge, one by one, from their private practice rooms where they have spent most of the day, ven-turing out only for meals. Once again their chosen school assumes its intended form as an institution of learning.

Right word?

Comment (Consensus: A)

   This theme is well-planned, and its plan is well-executed. The first paragraph both defines the central idea and establishes the method of its development by contrast and classification. The second and third paragraphs then describe two different types of students and the problems each presents, characterizing each group with fresh, concrete, and carefully chosen detail. In the fourth paragraph the writer considers one of the problems presented by the simultaneous presence of the two types, and in the final paragraph he returns to the contrast between weekday and Saturday students, effectively concluding his theme by exploiting at the same time the chronological pattern implicit in his topic. Each of his para-graphs is closely related to the central idea, and his transitions between paragraphs are smooth and effective. In addition, he develops the idea by a clearly apparent topic sentence. Although too many sentences begin with "There," the writer is, on the whole, skillful in giving variety and emphasis to his sentence-patterns. Similarly, his diction is often fresh and usually economical, but careful revision might have eliminated a few inaccuracies and ambiguities. In every other respect, this theme represents superior freshman writing.

In line with the "accent on the positive" approach to theme correcting is Lou LaBrant's chapter from her book, We Teach English. *All corrections must stimulate students to improve their writing, she insists, and advocates red underscoring of passages the teacher likes instead of the ones that need revising. Again, vagueness in a passage may be indicated by inviting the writer to explain inconsistencies by humorous or at least, good-humored comments. Neither should every student be required to revise every paper; indeed, criticism should be adapted to each individual in accordance with his "potential learning." In fine, careful marking, according to Miss LaBrant, is the "test of the teacher's own power of communicating."*

MARKING THE PAPER*

Lou L. LaBrant

And you take hold of a handle
by one hand or the other
by the better or worse hand
and you never know
maybe till long afterward
which was the better hand.

The People, Yes, Carl Sandburg[1]

The papers have been collected; they are yours to mark. What do you need to know, to consider, to do? Here is perhaps the most difficult test of teaching skill; for what you write on the student's paper should have more than one result. Will your comments lead him to write again, or to fear writing? Will they stimulate a desire to write better, or merely a fear of making errors? Will you be opening an exchange of understanding, or will you and the student communicate less and less from now on? What happens when the paper is returned, carrying your addition to the ideas expressed? How do you mark this paper?

It may be stated categorically that any good clerk can be taught to check usage, count errors, and produce a grade as valid as grades usually are; yet to many teachers marking means merely "correcting" and grading. Such an attitude is based on a most limited idea of what writing is about. Our student will need increased skill with structure, usage, and such forms as paragraphing, punctuation, placement of material on the page, neatness, and spelling; he will need to grow in ability to organize material, to use rhetorical devices. Unless, however, he wants to write, uses writing for significant purposes, and approaches writing with honesty and a sense of responsibility for what he says, it is hard to see why it matters whether or not his skill is increased. We have far too long wasted time and energy on polishing unimportant, meaningless, irresponsible writing. Marking the paper will encourage or discourage the acceptance of responsibility. The

*From Lou L. LaBrant, *We Teach English* (New York: Harcourt, Brace and Company, 1951), pp. 171-186. Used by permission of Lou L. LaBrant.

[1]Copyright, 1936, by Harcourt, Brace and Company, Inc. Reprinted by permission of the publisher.

question thus recurs: What is the teacher to do with this paper which his student
has handed to him?

First Requirement: Thoughtful Reading

The first step is to read the paper. This statement is not intended to be flip-
pant. Reading means giving thought to what is being said, seeing the paper as a
whole, reacting in terms of whatever has been done. If humanly possible, the
reading should be done first without marking unless the teacher can automatically
make check marks as he reads for ideas. (Experienced teachers can usually do
this; beginning teachers usually need two readings, one for ideas, and one for
usage, punctuation, and structure.) Reading should lead to some understanding
of what prompted the paper, what limited it, what its strengths and weaknesses
are, what it really says. After this reading the teacher is ready for comment. Certain issues have prime importance.

Criticism of Ideas

Obviously the first requirement is that the student be encouraged to continue
to express his ideas. Unless there are to be more papers, little learning will ensue.
This may not mean more writing on the same theme, but the present paper is a
step toward the next. Especially during the early weeks of the term, the teacher
must put forth unusual effort to encourage and suggest further communication.
What does this mean in practice? Certainly not to write baldly, "Continue" or
"Do another." Nor to praise insincerely what is not desirable. Students are quick
to sense this superficial attempt to stimulate writing. The most important stimulus
is to comment direct on the experiences put forth, even though these may be
relatively unimportant and feeble. If the student writes about a current political
issue, comment is easy; but the humble paper telling about a day in camp is another matter, more difficult because little is really revealed. Like a good conver-
sationalist, the teacher must pick up where the other left off. If the paper tells a
story, there may be a point at which the teacher can write "Amusing"; "Reminds
me of a drive my family once had along a dangerous stream"; "Many feel as you
do"; "This suggests another story you may want to write some day"; or "Do the
other boys and girls know why you came home?" Whatever the comment, it
should suggest respect for what the student has written, expectation of further
writing, and interest in the account. It should be mentioned at this point that a
writer is more influenced by attention than praise. There is a subtle compliment
even in disagreement: the writer is a person to be considered, else his ideas would
not matter to anyone. Such a comment as "This part seems to me beside the
point" implies clearly that the rest of the paper does have point or purpose or
value.

Sometimes a little device like the following is useful. A teacher who found that
his students were unusually fearful of teacher comment mentioned the first day
that as he read papers he had a habit of underscoring in red any sentence or

phrase which seemed to him unusually interesting or effective. (He used black for corrections.) Thus red marks, so often associated with failure, became quickly recognized evidences of the opposite. Needless to say, the teacher managed to find some spot for using the red line on most of the papers. The device permitted him to take advantage of even one or two well-chosen words.

Often, particularly when the first papers are weak and uninteresting, the teacher will be hard put to see in many of them anything worth a comment. There is the temptation to fall back on such remarks as "Good," "Interesting," or other empty praise; these remarks are to be avoided. They are to be avoided in the first place because they imply that the teacher's praise is of great importance. Good writing should not be done to please a teacher; good writing is an exchange of opinion, experience, emotion. It is essential to make clear to the student that the successful paper stimulates reaction in other people. This is a reason for having a paper by each student read in class early in the term. Often the teacher will write as much as the student. He will comment on an event by telling a little story of his own; he will ask questions, suggesting thereby a second paper; he will explain why some passage is not clear; he will ask for meanings. If this takes a great deal of time during the first weeks, it should be remembered that this is the season of the year when the teacher is most free for such work and that time spent then will be much more than repaid later in the year. As early as possible, responsibility for carrying on writing should be shifted to the shoulders of the students themselves. The teacher should not long have to motivate writing for most of the class.

Skillful comments will not only encourage further writing from the student but will lead to more significant topics. Let us say that the student, in perhaps the tenth grade, writes about picnics, hikes, or other rather trivial events, merely recounting the when, where, and obvious circumstances. A suggestion such as one of the following may be helpful: "Evidently you saw many things which you do not mention." "Are you a collector? Do you select your specimens?" "This picnic, *as you describe it*, seems like a thousand others. What happened that made you remember it? Was it something about the food, building the fire, or the friends you had with you? I don't think we understand." "Your story about the family trip leads me to think you and your parents enjoy doing things together, but I may be wrong. Could you let the rest of us know something about this?" "You mention liking to watch crowds in the station, but no two crowds are alike. What did you see? Weren't the people close enough to you that you could tell them apart? Surely you didn't just see them as a mass." "This event suggests that you were lonesome. When I am lonely I always feel sorry for myself and have a tendency to think about all the wrongs I've ever experienced."

The foregoing are very commonplace comments, but if you will examine them you will see that they are designed to dig a little deeper into the experience of the writer. Once faced with a real paper you will think of significant comments if you are really interested in the student and his writing.

Criticism of Writing

As the writing progresses, the comments will go into the character of the writing itself. Even young children in the junior high school often use words which have no clear meaning, and need to be brought to an understanding of how important it is that a person should know what he is writing about. "Labor," wrote a young high school student, evidently putting down what he had heard some adults say, "needs to be controlled." The teacher's comment was simply: "What do you mean by *labor*? Do you refer to all of the people who work, people like your father who is employed in an office? Do you mean teachers? Farmers? I am also not sure what you mean by 'controlled.' Do you mean that workers should be managed the way soldiers are managed? Could you make all of this clear?" The student finally recognized that he was using words without knowing what they meant. He wrote that this was so, and began to limit his pronouncements to simpler statements. Another student wrote about Jews. The teacher's note asked whether he meant people who had some ancestors who believed in the Jewish religion, or whether he meant people who themselves had a certain religious belief. The question sent the young writer to a series of discoveries. "Every kind of school work deserves rewards," wrote a ninth grade girl. She then drew the conclusion that students who make good grades should wear the felt letters usually awarded to athletes. The teacher called her attention to "award" and the need for explaining the word which she was using in two senses in the same discussion. As a result the girl spent considerable time exploring the nature of awards and rewards, with the result that her whole understanding — not to mention her paper — was greatly improved.

The illustrations just given are probably sufficient to show that, through comments, the teacher leads the student to explore new areas of experience and also to develop the areas already entered. Marking papers becomes in this way stimulating to both student and teacher. Nor need the markings be deadly in their seriousness. Amusing comments on inconsistencies, on implications, or on parallel experiences suggested by the account can make the reading of criticism pleasant. The total effect should, in most cases, be constructive. There are times, however, when it may be good medicine to suggest, "If I were you, I would throw this away and write something new."

Criticism of Form and Structure

Doubtless by this time some teacher is impatient to hear mention of "corrections." What do we do to errors in sentence structure, usage, spelling, and punctuation? Errors are, of course, not to be disregarded. Structure controls meaning, and until it is clear and suited to the writer's purpose there can be no clear communication. Punctuation likewise is a means towards clarity, but should not be considered until the basic pattern of the sentence is established. Punctuation, approved usage, conventional spelling, attractive placement on the page, and paragraphing are conventions, designed to make reading simpler and more pleasant.

Criticism of Meaning and Structure

If one or more sentences are confused, a first step in marking is to draw a line along the margin and write "Sentence Structure" (or "SS"), "Confused," "Meaning?" or any other expression which suggests that the writer has not said what he seems to be trying to say. Sometimes the problem is merely one of punctuation. Students should learn to recognize some abbreviation (possibly "P") as indicating this. Little is gained if the teacher indicates the correct point. The student has seen plenty of correct forms. He needs now to struggle for the form which clarifies his own thought. Sometimes sentences will be run together with no punctuation or perhaps a comma where a period should be used. A line under such a section with a marginal note may be effective. Write, for example, "This is run together. It does not make sense to me." Any child beyond the second grade knows that a declarative sentence should end with a period. *Finding where his sentence ends* is the difficulty. The student needs to struggle for the form which clarifies his own thought. This he will do if he is given two kinds of help: first, respect for his own piece; and second, time for the rewriting.

Usually even the more difficult structure problems are cleared up when the ideas are discussed with the student. The writer can clarify the sentence because *he knows what is intended.* Dangling clauses or phrases can be properly related as the one who has something to tell attempts to clarify his meaning in terms of a situation, real or imaginary, which is clear in his mind. It happens, of course, that sometimes there is no clear thought. Until the idea is clear, there can be no good writing.

It may be worth while here to recount an experience which throws some light on the important problem of the fragment, the uncompleted sentence. Almost every course of study and almost every composition book or workbook contains exercises designed to teach students to complete incomplete expressions. It seems strange that the idea has not occurred to teachers that the incomplete expression is evidence of a vague or confused experience and that it is unlikely to occur when the student is writing about something of major importance to him. Some years ago the writer of this book was attempting a study of sentence structure, and for that purpose needed the rapid natural writing of a thousand students. These ranged from early fourth through the twelfth grade. Since it seemed desirable to get rapid writing, separated in so far as possible from classroom controls the following method was used.

Most of the pupils were told that there had been considerable discussion concerning a longer school term — ten or eleven or more months instead of nine. They were asked what they thought of the idea and requested to write down their opinions hurriedly, since the questioner had only a short time. Eagerly the children wrote. They used pencils, yellow paper, and had no time for revision. When the resulting papers (averaging more than 150 words each) were studied, it was discovered that, although 20,000 clauses were written, there were only three fragments. This does not mean that there were no errors in punctuation and that such a sentence as "If you do this I will quit" was never cut in two by a period. But the full basic structure was there; only three from the thousands of sentences were unfinished. Why? The apparent answer is that the children had something important to say and, consequently, did not fail to finish statements they began. A youngster who thinks, as most of these did, that nine months of school is certainly a long stretch does not omit the main clause in writing "If you do this, *I will quit.*" Subesequent experience with teaching program where the writing was based largely on the child's own experience confirms the conclusion that if writing is clearly purposeful, if the writer knows what he has to say, the problem of the frequent error simply does not exist. There will, of course, be fragments deliberately used, but not omissions which leave the reader wondering.

The teacher should never forget that good structure is a reflection of the relationships in the mind of writer or speaker. A dependent clause should be used only when ideas call for one. There has been much false teaching that complex sentences should be introduced to provide variety of style. Style should never be subservient to truth: until one knows the relation between two statements he would do well to leave them as simple, independent units. Frequently, too, relationships seen by an adult are not recognized by the young writer. A teacher should consequently use great caution about suggesting changes which involve subordination.

Pronoun References

Junior high school students use many pronouns, and are beginning to have a difficulty which we all experience. Making some forty-odd words stand for all the nouns in the language is never easy. (One of the common errors found on the papers of graduate students is the pronoun without a clear antecedent.) The most direct correction is probably to underscore the faulty pronoun and write "Who?" in the margin. Sometimes instead the teacher chooses a reference he knows is wrong and writes "John?" being reasonably sure that John is not the one referred to. The purpose in any event is to call the attention of the writer to his lack of clarity and to point up the issue. This is usually more effective than sending him to a handbook for a rule about pronouns. "I cannot tell whether you mean John or Peter" is more easily understood than "There is a rule concerning pronoun reference to the effect that . . . ."

Spelling

The very bad speller is usually (some psychologists say always) a psychological problem. Frequently he is the child who has gained attention through bad spelling. Overanxious parents or teachers have made him so self-conscious that he cannot spell words he would otherwise handle easily. These severe cases should be given into the hands of a good psychologist where possible; but in no such case should the teacher emphasize the spelling. Often the simple method of ignoring spelling, and persuading parents to do so too for a three or four month period, will produce enormous gains. Bad spelling can be, and often is, an attention-getting device. "My mother spends hours helping me" is a warning to the teacher to avoid a similar method of rewarding the student for errors.

The reader should remember that the junior or the senior high school student has a vocabulary running into many thousands of words. Often overemphasis on spelling prevents his using most of those he knows. It is wise to accept as normal a considerable number of misspelled words, making the correction as easy as possible and taking for granted the obvious fact that ability to speak and to understand words runs far ahead of ability to spell them. There is no evidence that students are spelling less well today than students used to do; there is much evidence that students are trying to spell thousands of words which schools formerly never called for. Establish with the student the habit of putting into correct form all those papers which he thinks worth keeping and finishing, but do not be surprised and do not appear horrified if the young writer makes many spelling errors on his first drafts.

Adapting Criticism to the Individual

It should be evident to any thoughtful person that receiving criticism of one's writing can be a most discouraging experience. There is in every class the student whose paper is messy in appearance, or whose structure or spelling or usage is very poor. This is the student who dreads writing papers, and is unhappy the day they are returned. Frequently he is the least capable. He envies the "good" paper, the high mark of the student across the aisle. The situation seems very unfair to him. There sits the complacent owner of the perfect paper, faced with no corrections; here he sits, confused, unskilled with language, faced with twenty errors. Obviously he has before him more work than the capable student, and obviously also he is not likely to learn much as he struggles with twenty bad spots in his paper. He would do well if he really understood and corrected four. This is just what he should be allowed to do. It is poor teaching to demand what the teacher knows cannot be done. Corrections, suggestions for revision, and criticisms of content should be given in proportion to the ability of the student to use them. They are means to improvement, not penalties for being dull or inexperienced or incompetent. Therefore, as the teacher indicates errors in usage, he will keep in mind the writer and his abilities. This may mean overlooking all but the most glaring errors; it may mean more help for the weak student; it may also, as will be indicated later, mean an adjustment in requirements for rewriting.

Teachers sometimes say that all students should be treated alike. If an error is marked for one, it should be for another. The word "alike" can apply to many relations. Treating all with like care may mean very different handling of two papers. No one would argue that treating all children "alike" meant dressing them all in suits of the same size. If the marks on papers are limited to errors, the procedure invites comparison. If, however, suggestions are understood as means to ends, if there are copious notes dealing with the communication as such, the teacher is free to mark in terms of the potential learning of the student.

Rewriting the Papers

Revision is the next step. Probably not all papers need rewriting, but many do. A time for this work should be set aside in the regular class periods. This permits conferences, time for approving corrected or revised papers and help in working out difficult problems. If instead of attempting to rearrange the student's sentence, or to check each misplaced or undesirable form, the teacher has indicated difficulty by such terms as "Confusion," "Lack of punctuation," "Word order," or "Awkward," if there are passages underscored, with the words "Not clear" in the margin, the problem of making better statements will be thrown back on the writer. His first step may be to talk over with the teacher or a classmate what it was he meant to say. If the whole paper calls for more effort than the student seems able to give, one paragraph or page may be selected and only this section cleaned up. Spelling may be corrected without rewriting an entire page. If the teacher's corrections have been made in pencil there is a possibility that simple corrections may be made, the comments erased, and the paper approved for filing.

For the more competent student there are questions of better organization, suggestions for sections which may be sharpened, perhaps a chance to write an added paper. There is no need that everyone in the class should produce an identical number of papers any more than there is need that everyone should write papers of identical length. We make absurd demands for quantity, much as though a hostess were to assign to each guest the length of time he might talk. Some students write freely, and yet are not the best writers. Some write short, compact statements, characteristic of their general behavior. The most prolific writers in our century are not necessarily our greatest.

Giving a Grade

Discussion of marking papers has not dealt with grades, those inadequate measures which we teachers have so firmly established to our own undoing. Early in the term it is well to discuss grades if they are to be given and, in any event, to set up with the students values to be considered. Some of these may be the neatness and correct form of papers, or the punctuality of the student in writing and revising work. Other values, more difficult to appraise, may be clarity, interest, effectiveness, depth, sincerity, or variety of the papers. All of these being considered, what is the degree of improvement? Comparing the student's attempts in September to his work in January or June, do we see some gain? Has he, perhaps, attempted to write verse or short stories, whereas he once wrote merely descriptions or narratives of personal doings? Does he rewrite more intelligently now than at first? Whatever the values set, the year's folders, with the faulty originals and the neat, approved final drafts, all can come out for inspection during the last week of the semester or the year. There will be some thin folders, some unrevised efforts, probably some obvious gains. In conference between student and teacher, a mark can be decided. No one should believe that this grade is absolute, perfect, or altogether just. But it makes more sense than the arbitrary grade, based on tests, number of errors, and the length of the paper. It goes without saying that there is something more intelligent to be done in evaluation than using a letter or a figure. Many schools have substituted reports which really tell both student and parent about what has been going on at school. It is a strange commentary on communication skills in many schools that teachers — the teacher of composition included — can find nothing more coherent to say about a young student and his exploration of ideas than "B" or "A" or perhaps "D."

There is no magic formula for marking papers; the teacher must take the writing of a growing youngster who is attempting what is perhaps the hardest thing a human being can do (to organize his own thinking and record that on paper) — the teacher must consider this writing and along with it the writer, and make in an imperfect way the most helpful comments he can devise. Marking papers thus becomes a severe test of the teacher's own power of communication. Here is no mechanical process, rather, here is a test of the competence of the teacher of English to demonstrate the skill he teaches.

Teachers who insist on marking every error in every student composition should ask themselves whether such an all-out attack really works. Paul Diederich believes it does not, and in this essay he suggests an approach to annotating papers which is selective, positive, and humane.

IN PRAISE OF PRAISE*

PAUL B. DIEDERICH

The average English paper corrected by the average English teacher looks as though it had been trampled on with cleated boots and has about the same effect on the student. I realize that some good-hearted teachers believe that this savagery is necessary, just as "practical schoolmen" a hundred years ago knew for certain that the only way to teach a boy Latin was to whip him.

I believe that many English teachers have a false theory about how to get rid of those pesky little errors that disfigure most student writing. They seem to think that drowning them in red ink will do away with them.

The only trouble with this approach is that it doesn't seem to work. The results of a recent series of grammar and usage tests given each level of college preparatory students in one of the oldest public high schools on the Eastern seaboard indicated that errors were being eliminated at the rate of about 2 percent a year. Chances are these errors would probably have declined at about this rate if English teachers had ignored them.

I am strongly tempted to believe, although I have no way of proving it, that all this outpouring of red ink not only does no good but positive harm. Its most common effect is to make the majority of students hate and fear writing. So far as they can see, they have never done anything on paper that anybody thought was good. No matter how hard they try, every paper they hand in gets slapped down for something or other.

The art of the teacher — at its best — is the reinforcement of good things. I am reminded of an experience from my own college days. I had one of the original "theme-a-day" courses at Harvard, taught at that time by Professor Hurlbut. So far as I can remember, he practically never said anything bad about our papers. About two or three times in an average paper we did something that was worthy of praise. We usually knew it, and his comment invariably indicated that he knew it, too. The space between these high points in our papers was filled with the usual student bilge, which he never honored with a comment. Whenever he said nothing, we knew that the verdict was "undistinguished" but that he was too much of a gentleman to say so.

About all Professor Hurlbut ever did in class was to read papers that he regarded as unusually good, without telling us who had written them. We sat there gasping, wishing that we had written them ourselves. He seldom stopped to say what was good about these papers. We either knew it, or his voice told us. In rare cases he might ask, "Now what was particularly good about that?"

---

*Paul B. Diederich, "In Praise of Praise," NEA Journal, LII (Stepember 1963), 58-59. Used by permission of Paul B. Diederich and NEA Journal, Mildred S. Fenner, Editor.

I cannot remember a single instance in which he ever asked what was bad about a paper. For him to express dispraise was as rare as for him to lose his temper — which was almost inconceivable.

I believe that a student knows when he has handed in something above his usual standard and that he waits hungrily for a brief comment in the margin to show him that the teacher is aware of it, too. To my mind, these are the only comments that ever do any student any good.

Up to this point, I must have given readers the impression that there is no place whatever for brutality in the treatment of student writing. Actually, there is a place for it, when it is used in the following way: Duplicate and pass out to your class one student paper on each assignment. Use an anonymous paper from a different class, so that the students who criticize it may be sure that the writer will not be present to have his feelings hurt.

Have the students study this paper as homework, grade it, and mark it up with every sort of criticism and suggestion for improvement. Next day in class, let them argue over their grades and suggestions.

During this session everything bad that can be said about a paper ought to be said, and you may count on the students to say it. You may even have to defend the paper against an unjustified attack.

Since these sessions are an exercise in criticism, I think the sample papers should be of all kinds: good, bad, and indifferent. Some teachers balk at this idea, holding that students should never see an example of admittedly poor writing lest it corrupt them. I answer them by pointing out that the way students write is the result of hearing the language used imperfectly sixteen hours a day, every day of their lives. One more instance of imperfect language, recognized as such, and followed up by devastating criticism, is not going to corrupt them more than they have been corrupted already.

I believe that student papers should be dealt with something like this:

Find in each paper at least one thing, and preferably two or three things, that the student has done well, or better than before. Then, if you must, find one thing, and preferably not more than one thing, that he should try to improve in his next paper. Whenever possible make this a suggestion, not a prescription.

Learning one new thing per paper is certainly more than most students learn at present. As for the other ninety-nine errors that disfigure the paper and disgrace the school, simply ignore them. If you mark them all, or even half of them, the student learns nothing; he only advances one step further toward a settled conviction that he can't write and there is no use trying.

If you pursue my suggested policy, a few parents may bring student themes to school, point angrily to errors they recognize, and ask why they were overlooked. You can easily work out of this jam by indicating a few of the flaws that the parent has overlooked, telling him that no student could possibly learn that much about writing from a single paper, and pointing out that you have carefully selected one weakness for the student to try to eliminate in his next paper.

If a student concentrates on one error at a time, progress is possible; if he tries to overcome all of his weaknesses at once, he will only be overwhelmed. I do not know where the scientific truth lies, but I have more faith in the value of a few appreciative comments than in any amount or kind of correction.

One day, I descended the stairs in my longest skirt, knee high socks, loafers, and my red, bulky turtle-neck sweater. My paternal grandmother was sitting primly on our pink flowered chair, sipping a cup of tea. As I walked into the room, I thought she was going to spit the tea all over the wall. *Lovely choice of details*

Shattering contrast!

"Beverly!" she screamed to my mother. "Beverly, you must do something about this child. Why, the way she dresses is obscene! Just look at the length of her skirt." *well-chosen word In character.*

Her face was red and purple-striped, and since I had never seen her in such a rage, I became rather frightened.

Splendid! Sounds just like her. "Why, when I was a girl, if I had worn that outfit, people would have suspected that I was of questionable morals. Why don't you buy that girl some high-button shoes and black stockings?"

My mother tried to calm her by saying, "Now, now, mother, that is the fashion of the times, you know."

"Pshaw!" answered my grandmother and tottered grandly out of the room. *Some would say that one cannot totter grandly; but I think grandma could. Like Charles De Gaulle.* I think the trouble with families is that they are not up with the times, but I have no time to prove it. It takes me too long to button up those high-button shoes.

A snapper of an ending! Very effective to leave it like this — without putting in the intervening steps.

You make grandma come to life. A few bold strokes, and everything in character.

PB Diederich *A!*

For the teachers with too great a paper load, Sarah Roody offers practical household hints — while every paper should be filed, not every one need be corrected, returned and revised. In Miss Roody's plan, what students have learned and appreciate is that the few they do get back each semester are marked "thoroughly and personally"; they are made aware of weaknesses, yet are conscious, too, of progress. When themes are written on class time, the marking is done on the spot. Finally, the employment of a student "committee" to assist in composition correction makes the task of grading more meaningful for teacher and pupils — all of whom are at some time a part of the "committee" of student "lay readers." Miss Roody stresses the fact that this plan was an emergency measure resorted to when she was teaching 150 pupils and more. When she has lighter pupil loads, she gives each paper much thoughtful attention and many marginal comments.

MANAGING STUDENT WRITING[*]

Sarah I. Roody

My system of handling written work is organized around the belief that the personal touch makes the task more interesting and that methodical procedures make it easier. The waves of frustration that used to engulf me when I saw my desk piled high with compositions drove me to search for a method of making the accumulation smaller, of keeping it organized, and of grading the papers in such a way as to get the best results possible from a reasonable amount of work. Bit by bit I have evolved a system.

I handle the papers no more than necessary. Pupils alphabetize them as they are handed in, and then I place the set in a dated folder and put it into the drawer of my filing cabinet where I keep all ungraded papers. I file the papers of each class separately.

Each time I take papers from a class I notice whether anyone has failed to submit one, and make a notation in my class book. When a student hands in a late paper, he drops it into a basket on my desk. Since nearly every paper bears a heading indicating at the right the student's name and course division and at the left the date and the nature of the assignment, I can easily file each one properly and give its writer credit for submitting it.

The knowledge that every paper is saved and that I can place my hand on any given paper at a moment's notice tends to discourage pupils from being unprepared and from handing in incomplete papers.

Written work is done about once a week. Three or four of the papers prepared by each student during a semester of nineteen weeks I mark thoroughly and personally. On each of those papers I write notes analyzing the student's skills and his weaknesses, explaining his errors, and commenting on his progress. The nature of the note varies.

---

*Sarah I. Roody, "Managing Student Writing," *English Journal*, XLIV (February 1955), 75-79. Used by permission of Sarah I. Roody.

To an average student I explain each type of serious error he has made and point out every instance; for example, I tell him why two thoughts expressed in a certain sentence are parallel and how he can cast them in parallel constructions. Then I bracket each subsequent passage in need of parallelism and write a notation such as "Show by use of parallelism that these statements are both reasons." Many of the notations are very short.

To a brilliant student dealing with complex ideas I may write, "Your vocabulary is broad and varied and you are learning to say exactly what you mean. When explaining a difficult point use shorter sentences and avoid interrupting one thought with another. Revise the bracketed passages. Find and correct two comma splices, one fragment, and dangling participle. Review uses of commas and punctuate your paper. With suitable corrections it will be worth 90. Now it rates about 80."

My comments to a weak student are less demanding and more explanatory. I criticize only the errors he is capable of correcting, and I sometimes limit my criticisms to only one type of error.

Papers graded in this way are likely to be short ones. Long compositions are often handed back with only a grade and a note.

Although I can do highly personalized marking only a few times a semester, I employ certain expedients between times.

When composition work is done in class, I grade the papers as they are being written. Keeping clearly in mind exactly what I am looking for and what qualities make a composition excellent, good, adequate, or poor, I move from desk to desk and look for certain elements on each round. Does the pupil have in mind a definite idea to be developed and a clear plan of development? His outline (if he makes one) and his first sentence answer these questions for me. Does he proceed to develop fully and coherently the thought he has introduced, or does he merely pick up and lay down several ideas in turn? Does his paragraph division indicate the steps in his development? Does the ending interpret what he has said about his topic? Of course I am continually evaluating sentence structure, wording, paragraph structure, and mechanics of expression. If the paper is not a test, I point out the weaknesses and errors to the student and tell him to remedy them. Each time I look at a student's paper, I evaluate what he has written, and I may change his grade several times as I continue on my rounds. Usually, however, a student who has a clear purpose in mind also develops his central point well and arranges his material coherently. One who constructs his sentences clearly often words them precisely. Grading may be difficult, however, when originality and faulty mechanics appear on the same paper. If the pupil fails to correct the mechanical errors pointed out to him, his originality is not enough to guarantee him a high grade.

Although I have learned to grade papers rather accurately while they are being written, grades given in that way are likely to be higher than usual. Another method yielding grades sometimes a bit too high but nevertheless producing some definitely desirable results is letting student committees grade papers under my supervision. Answers to questions on literature offer excellent material for this method.

The committee members and I discuss what the content of the answer should be and how much credit should be allotted to each required informational item and to the quality of the composition. Each committee member writes an answer, I write a detailed evaluation on each of those answers, and all committee members read all my comments. My grades and instructions guide the committee in grading the papers of the rest of the class. (The theme readers themselves are graded on their judgment in evaluating the papers.) Before the papers are returned to their owners, I read them and rectify any serious errors made by the committee. Some time during the year every student who keeps his own work above average has an opportunity to serve on such a committee. This method is successful only if I have worded the questions clearly in the first place and have formulated a definite criterion in my own mind so that I can give practicable instructions to the committee and demonstrate my own instructions in grading their answers.

I do not grade every paper submitted by each student, but I keep all unmarked papers in the file. About once a week I read the ungraded papers of four or five students and record in my class book one grade for each of those students — a progress grade. Before report cards go out I also refer to the ungraded papers of pupils about whom I may feel uncertain. Later in the year ungraded papers are also utilized when I assign class work on finding and correcting errors.

You may offer the objection that my system requires a great deal of forethought. It does. Let me also admit here and now that it does not develop all of my students into effective writers. It does, however, help to create interest in writing. Its strongest recommendations are that it almost completely does away with feeling of confusion and futility caused by keeping in sight piles of ungraded and unorganized papers, that it convinces the pupils their papers are not ignored even when they are not graded, that it strengthens personal relations between teacher and pupils, and that it also leads to greater development of the students' skills in composition than any other plan that I have been able to use with large numbers of students.

In this article, excerpted from the longer one in the English Journal *of October, 1955, Mr. Dusel advocates a trend away from the use of conventional symbols in marking themes. Instead, he says, where clarity is lacking, for example, the teacher should ask simple questions in the manner of the "friendly reader who wants to understand." In avoiding symbols which often, regrettably, say more for the troubled adolescent than was intended, teachers remove what constitute obstacles to reaching the pupil as a person. At the same time, however, the truth must be told; but it should be done a little at a time. To emphasize thought in one marking and mechanics in another removes, in part, "the sting of correction" and enables the student to perfect his skills one at a time.*

SOME SEMANTIC IMPLICATIONS OF THEME CORRECTION*

William J. Dusel

In an attempt to discover the cause for weak writing found in high school graduates, the California Council of English Associations sponsored a statewide study of the teaching of writing in California secondary schools. More than 400 experienced teachers, representing 150 different communities throughout the state, contributed their ideas on the way writing should be taught, described the working conditions under which they must teach it, and sent in examples of their marking and grading techniques. The great body of opinions, reports, and samples of work which were collected for analysis has given the California Council unusual perspective in identifying the problems which confront teachers of writing in California secondary schools. It has also made clear some of the directions in which improvement lies. That the sampling was of more than local significance is indicated by the fact that the teachers who participated in the study had received their professional training in thirty different states and the Dominion of Canada.

Suggestions for Marking

One fact established by the Council survey helps explain why English teachers mark papers as they do: it takes three times as long to analyze a theme for ideas and organization and signs of improvement, and to comment on these, as to check it for mechanics alone. Until teachers are given a lighter pupil load and are provided with daily marking periods as part of their assigned schedule, they cannot be expected to read carefully and mark effectively the recommended amounts of writing practice. Meanwhile, conscientious teachers will give each pupil as much practice in purposeful writing as their teaching load permits them to supervise. The following suggestions may be helpful to those who wish to make more cleanly communicative whatever marking they can find time to do.

SHOW APPRECIATION OF SUCCESSFUL WRITING. An excellent paper which is returned to a pupil practically untouched may not seem as successful to the writer

---

*From William J. Dusel, "Some Semantic Implications of Theme Correction," *English Journal*, XLIV (1955), 390. Used by permission of William J. Dusel.

as the teacher intends it to seem. The pupil has no way of knowing whether unmarked parts of his writing have been read or not. There is real need to develop as many symbols of appreciation and enjoyment as of dissatisfaction.

The words of praise — "good," "excellent," even "wonderful!" — are useful, but being adjectives of judgment rather than of description, they rarely indicate the point of excellence. They should be followed by the appropriate substantives, so that the writer knows both what was good about his writing and also what made it good. With that additional information he may be better able to repeat the success in his next composition.

Writing the word "yes" occasionally in the margin is an excellent way of letting the writer know that the reader is nodding his head in agreement or understanding. For variety the teacher might comment with "I agree" or "true" or even "You're so right."

One of the most effective, but most time-consuming, forms of appreciative response is the teacher's amplification of the pupil's idea. Such a sign of respect and acceptance may assure the writer of the genuine interest of the teacher more effectively than can any letter grade, including the "A+."

EMPHASIZE THE IMPORTANCE OF PURPOSE AND IDEA IN WRITTEN COMPOSITION. Teachers who sincerely believe that the ideas which the pupil wishes to communicate are more important than the mechanics of expression can make their values known by the way they mark. If faulty mechanics must be pointed out, teachers can show how the error distorts or clouds the meaning. If a modifier is misplaced, they can indicate the ludicrous meaning conveyed and ask if that was the one intended. If the antecedent of a pronoun is missing or indeterminable, they can use the comment attributed to the late Harold Ross: "Who he?" Such a question focuses the writer's attention on meaning; whereas conventional symbols like "ref" or "faulty antecedent" seem to criticize on technical grounds that only English teachers consider important.

In general, rather than name errors, teachers might do better to ask questions — questions which the pupil, through inexperience or negligence, raises in the mind of a friendly reader who wants to understand.

Some teachers try to achieve a desired balance between comments on ideas and concern for mechanics by reacting to the former in the left margin, to the latter on the right of each page. This technique makes startlingly graphic the average teacher's tendency to neglect content as he marks.

One of the most promising methods of marking to emphasize idea involves the limiting of comments on pupils' compositions to interested responses to ideas only. Errors of mechanics, diction, and sentence structure are noted on separate record cards kept by the teacher. To process a pupil's composition, the teacher reads it through twice. The first time he looks only for the kinds of errors which he and the class have decided are taboo at that grade level. Each error observed is recorded as a tally mark in the appropriate column of the pupil's record card. Words misspelled are listed at the bottom of the card. In the second reading (the most time-consuming one) the teacher considers the ideas which the writer is attempting to express, and comments in the margin on these ideas and on the progress shown by the writer — a completely positive kind of criticism. After checking the writing of his pupils in this way for several weeks, the teacher will be able to see, from the frequency distribution of tally marks, the kinds of remedial instruction and drill needed by each pupil. He then can either assign section of a workbook for individual study or discuss in general class session the difficulties common to all. Keeping such a complete record of the errors of each pupil enables the teacher to bring to the writer's attention only as many points as should be considered at one time, without losing the opportunity to refer eventually to the rest of the weaknesses.

After the pupils have studied and drilled on their special problems, they are given their tally cards and their folder of compositions and are asked to find and correct all the kinds of errors they have been studying. In this way each pupil proofreads material of his own creation; and because he has been prepared to view his past writing in a new, more critical light, he can appreciate the value of his remedial work and see the progress he has made.

This procedure, because it separates the fault-finding from the free exchange of ideas which should characterize the English class, seems promising. The pupil's composition — an unselfconscious effort to communicate an important idea to a respected person — is returned in something of the same spirit in which it is offered, with comments on the significance, the implications, the uniqueness or universality of the writer's thoughts. Repair work is undertaken whenever the writer has been convinced, by the growing satisfaction he receives from being understood and appreciated, that accurate writing is worth the trouble.

INDICATE FAULTS IN SUCH A WAY AS TO FACILITATE LEARNING. Many teachers mark compositions apparently on the assumption that a person who has his mistakes pointed out to him will thereby be made anxious to correct those mistakes. Others assume that a grade will serve as an incentive to further effort. While still others must imagine that their own corrections of a pupil's mistakes will prepare him to write correctly next time. Teachers who are familiar with the laws of learning, with the importance of motive and emotion and activity and insight, will be perfectly aware of the unreliability of these three forms of marking as guides or spurs to learning.

A pupil's errors must, of course, be brought to his attention. But finding fault with a young person without losing his friendship, or more important, without killing his interest in writing, is work too delicate and difficult to entrust to crude, wildly connotative symbols — marks that say more than the teacher intends. The eternal problem of the teacher of writing is how to remove the sting of correction, how to lessen the chagrin of the adolescent who has revealed his ignorance. The teacher can never be certain of the writer's ability to take criticism of anything as personal as his language, his thoughts actually his personality.

Getting pupils to judge their own work on clearly defined standards which have been accepted by the group enables the teacher to identify beforehand many of those who are likly to be upset by unfavorable criticism. Pupils who are unrealistic in appraising their work need counsel, if they are to be kept teachable, before the teacher grades them.

Offering the noncommittal word "interesting" in response to some adolescent's untenable but firm conviction is the kind of respectful response that keeps lines of communication open for later, more complete and enlightened discussion.

Teachers should usually refrain from putting a low grade on a student's composition if they expect that the grade may have a depressing effect on him. He is more in need of knowing how to improve his work than of being reminded that he has failed. An "F" is concrete, immutable. It's in the records and, what's worse, in the pupil's mind. It will not be washed away by kind words and helpful comments. The pupil may not even be able to hear, or at least really understand, subsequent explanations and suggestions. Teachers of English might well consider paraphrasing the safety rule of the rifle range ("Never point a gun at anything you do not intend to kill") to read "Never put the mark of failure on the work of any person you do not intend to hurt." In day-to-day evaluation, the absence of a grade is safer communication than a mark of failure. This is not to say that there must be no judging of failure; but only that in evaluation short of the final reckoning, no worthy purpose is served with most pupils by branding their unsuccessful efforts with a scarlet "F."

Teachers who wish to help *all* their pupils to become better writers and who have some clear ideas on how to teach writing will try to mark so as to be understood perfectly. They will acquire a strong distrust of letter grades and monosyllabic comments, remembering the unpredictable power of many of these traditional symbols to mislead or upset the young person. They will depend more on carefully phrased sentences, directed to the individual writer. And some day, when lightened teaching loads permit, they will teach writing even more effectively through teacher-pupil conferences.

Those teachers who interpret all this concern for the feelings of learners as molly-coddling may feel that such care as has been suggested to keep interest in writing alive is ridiculous. They may recount the shocks they themselves have withstood from their own teachers who never hesitated to call a spade a spade: "And it made a man of me!" they will conclude. The ability of the strong to survive rough treatment, however, does not justify inefficient teaching. The loss is with the weak — those who lose heart and quit trying, those who decide prematurely that college is not for them, the majority who leave school unable to write a clear, grammatical, spirited, friendly letter. Mass education in a democracy must strengthen the weak, not eliminate them. And the average pupil requires careful handling, at least until he has found his own reasons for wanting to learn to write.

Following a detailed and individual breakdown of some familiar postulates on composition writing and correction, Mr. Levine asserts that unless the student has access to reading numerous papers written by his "peers," he has no real norm of comparison for judging the worth of his own theme writing — he has this need just as does a teacher who sees each student's theme in relation to the other hundreds of themes he reads weekly. By the use of three examples, the author then illustrates how theme reading, together with the use of specific questions as guides to appreciation and attention to all the aspects of composition excellence, should eventuate in greater understanding of the rules and, ultimately, in better writing.

FROM GUIDED THEME READING TO IMPROVED WRITING*

Isidore Levine

A radical change in composition instruction is long overdue on all levels of our school system. It is true we have come a long way from the first attempts to discipline the expression of thoughts transferred to paper. However, our present problems of method in composition and our knowledge of psychology should inspire us to make the effort to examine some of our basic premises in language teaching.

Today the struggles of the teacher of composition, with his ever increasing pile of unmarked papers, have unearthed quite a number of suggested solutions. But few of these panaceas are seriously considered by the majority of those most intimately affected by the problem — the classroom teachers. Perhaps the Conant Report, the Rutgers Plan sponsors, and the Commission on English may eventually promote the sweeping changes in administration foreseen as the ultimate necessity. But, in the meanwhile, we can and should study new approaches to composition work which do not contemplate the special difficulties lay readers create, or the organizational revolution the Rutgers Plan proposes, or the illusory Utopianisms (the four teaching periods and 100 students program) Dr. Conant and the Commission demand.

Postulates of Composition Teaching

Our present practices in composition instruction are based on a number of postulates which should be carefully reviewed.

1. We should review the idea that pupils can learn to write their one to six paragraph themes and letters by guided reading of the literature studied in the classroom — this despite the fact that none of the short stories, poems, novels, biographies, essays, or plays resembles the simple models of brevity of thought and content that characterize the student product.

2. We should determine the value of grammar. There is a body of knowledge called grammar which each teacher of language arts possesses. She can

---

*From Isidore Levine, "Teach Students to Be Their Own Lay Readers," *High Points*, XLVI, 2 (February 1964), 21-37. Used by permission of Isidore Levine and *High Points*, A. Ponemon, Edito r.

teach her students to learn and apply it, and she can use it herself in correcting pupil work. The structural linguists, basing their studies on the spoken, rather than the written, word are challenging this premise. Whether the results of their researches will ultimately convince the teacher is questionable. However, there is no doubt that the structuralists are throwing some much needed light on this traditional view.

3. We should find out whether the correct identification and practice of the linguistic forms and techniques of grammar can be translated from textbook knowledge into the realities of individual expression. We find an increasing number of teachers accepting the truth of such statements as Dr. Mersand's in the April 1961 *English Journal,* "A good textbook in composition and rhetoric may be used for reference and occasional exercises but for little else." Much research is needed to determine the value of the classroom procedures concerned with that "little else," procedures justified by the persuasive influence of the theory of transfer of training.

4. We must ask ourselves, "Does the teacher time spent in encircling, underlining, or overwriting the variety of errors and expressional weaknesses betrayed by students benefit the young writer?" Nowhere do we find any evidence of the value of such corrections in any studies of such efforts made by teachers doing the work. It is the lack of such evidence that has enabled the recommendations of Dr. Conant and others to go unchallenged. Tradition dictates the necessity for red-pencilling; therefore the exorbitant amount of time needed for such activity is to be decreased by assigning a teacher a maximum of 100 students, or hiring a lay reader, or limiting the number of compositions the teacher is himself to read.

5. We must investigate whether pupils can be taught the value of words in expressing thoughts vividly and exactly through a variety of vocabulary exercises. The secondary school language books abound in such developmental language activities as the following: derivation of words, synonyms and antonyms, context clues, word notebooks, study of prefixes and suffixes, dictionary exercises, and analyses of unidiomatic expressions. Again there is little beyond a faith in transfer of learning to prove that such experiences can make more articulate writers of our youngsters.

Reasons for Abandoning Traditional Methods

An examination of these five premises provides the elements of a new approach to composition illustrated in this paper.

1. In addition to the literary selections read as models of good writing, pupils need to study scores of compositions of their peers, under teacher guidance. Appreciation of the superior and inferior qualities of their own written products can be developed most effectively through analysis of such pupil writings rather than through careful observation of the perfections of the literary masters beyond their reach. This program of dissection entails much more than mere perusal and grading of a neighbor's paper, as will be seen below.

2. We do not have a standard body of linguistic forms and usages based on the achievement levels of high school students. Our language texts and manuals of writing are compendia of writings of approved authors, who provide the descriptions of accepted English and hundreds of isolated instances of faulty communication which furnish the bases for the prescriptive rules to correct such errors. We need an analysis of hundreds of complete themes, such estimates as are suggested by the pamphlets of the Illinois Association of Teachers of English, *Evaluating Ninth Grade Themes* and *Evaluating Twelfth Grade Themes*. No collection of that kind exists to provide material for a study of the standards expected of high school students, despite the millions of compositions discarded weekly during the school year.

3. Lessons in grammar and technique which treat some isolated fault, (e.g., sentence fragment, misuse of the comma, unidentified pronoun antecedents) although logical in theory, are not productive of the desired precision, even though the pupil may have a working knowledge of the rules. Each element of writing requiring specific instruction should be based on the actual context of a complete theme rather than on the microscopic specimen of a mistake which pinpoints its own correction when removed from the living organism that is the unedited essay. This point may be further clarified in the actual explorations below.

4. An examination of the variety of pamphlets on composition evaluation reveals the sweeping gamut of corrective possibilities in which a composition reader can indulge. The Spring 1958 bulletin of the Michigan Council of Teachers of English, entitled *Evaluating a Theme*, is a case in point. The 25 responses from high school and college teachers in answer to a request for the appraisal of a student theme represent the manifold practices of thousands of teachers of English. Yet the improvement the pupil could register if he read all the comments both studiously and eagerly is still to be determined.

We assume the pupil grasps the meaning of the suggestions such as those offered by the experts. Yet it is extremely doubtful that even our bright youngsters can interpret practically such estimates as these:
   a. Writer shows a real effort to organize
   b. Theme did not follow outline
   c. Good conclusion except for shift of person in the last sentence
   d. The final paragraph is a flat summation which despite is pseudo-humorous rhetorical question does not, as I see it, constitute a "good ending."
   e. Awkward bunt transition
   f. Avoid passive if possible
   g. Although "wise up" is in quotation marks, I object to the use of slang in a serious, informative paper.
   h. An excellent introduction
   i. The opening episode does not seem to introduce the problem.

All the above remarks are taken from the Michigan bulletin previously noted. The contradictions are deliberately chosen. However, if the pupil were not shown these sharp differences, he would still be in the position described by Dr. Roberts in his book *Understanding English*:

> But the question of whether writing is dull or interesting is a matter of opinion, and the instructor's opinion is the only one that counts. The student cannot judge his own writing. He sees it by itself and has nothing against which to measure it. A teacher sees it against thousands of other student compositions and actually has very little difficulty in deciding whether it is, in comparison, good, bad, or average. (*Understanding English* — Paul Roberts, Harpers, 1958, page 8.)

Of what help is the advice "awkward blunt transition" to a student writer unfamiliar with the scores of smooth logical paragraph shifts the critic teacher has perused and judged? How will the pupil benefit from the recommendation to "avoid the passive if possible" if he has not learned the value of the active verb and the appropriate use of the passive through reading and assessing hundreds of examples of each?

Other facets of this traditional practice of red-inking errors in a paper can be discussed, but, to the writer, it seems plain that what the pupil needs is the experience of reading many papers written by his peers, so that he can understand and judge his own work with that knowledge as a basis.

5. At present, teachers and text writers relate their vocabulary exercises to the uses of a dictionary with its isolated word meanings often lacking clear relationship. The peculiar problems of expression confronting a writer can hardly be solved by a dictionary. Thus a pupil who uses *like* repeatedly because he cannot think of another word, although he feels that other phrases might be more suitable, would find these items in a dictionary:

   a. *Thorndike Century Junior Dictionary*
      like — Boys like to play. Baby likes milk. Mother knows all my likes and dislikes.
   b. Funk and Wagnall's *Standard H.S. Dictionary of the English Language*
      like—1. to incline favorably toward; to be pleased with; as "every one likes him" 2. to please; choose; as "do as you like"
   c. *Winston Dictionary* — Intermediate Edition (1945)
      like — v.t. — 1. to have a taste for; enjoy; find agreeable 2. to wish or want v.i. to choose; as do as you like n. in pl., the thing one enjoys or prefers

Other dictionaries would furnish similar limited uses for the writer. We are supposing that the student is able to interpret the special language of dictionaries.

The thesaurus is the appropriate book to use to roam the fields of expression in language. Thus for *like*, the thesaurus (Edition 1933—American) provides this comprehensive listing:

like — similar (17) relish (394) enjoy (377, 837) wish (865) love (898) do what one likes (748) look like (448) we shall not look upon his like again (33) like master like man (19)

Each number in the parenthesis refers to a special, numbered paragraph which furnishes a variety of synonyms and substitutes followed by a succeeding paragraph of antonyms and opposites. Roget's *Pocket Thesaurus* lists the following for 377:

377. Physical pleasure N. pleasure, bodily enjoyment, animal gratification, gusto, relish, delight, sensual delight, sensuality; luxuriousness, dissipation, round of pleasure; comfort, ease, luxury, lap of luxury; creature comforts; purple and fine linen; bed of roses

treat; diversion, entertainment, banquet, refreshment feast.

happiness, felicity, bliss, beatitude,

V. enjoy, relish; luxuriate in, revel in, bask in, wallow in; feast on, gloat over, smack the lips

please, charm, delight, enchant, etc. (829)

Adj. comfortable, cosy, snug, in comfort, at ease, luxurious, in clover, **agreeable** etc. (829); grateful, refreshing, comforting, cordial, genial; gratifying, sensuous; palatable, delicious, sweet; fragrant; melodious, harmonious; lovely, etc. (845)

Adv. in comfort, on a bed of roses, on flowery beds of ease

As can be seen, the thesaurus gives a much more realistic picture of the vistas of our language than does any dictionary. When a student needs more vivid and exact words, he should be able to select the expressions English provides in the rich storehouse of language borrowings and additions the centuries have established. Lessons based on the specific vocabulary problems of a high school writer are self-motivated and most practical. It is true that time must be spent on teaching the use of the thesaurus. But these hours can be taken from the periods now devoted to the routine exercises listed above.

Using Student Compositions

Getting down to specifics, the methods advocated to teach pupils to become their own lay readers is outlined in the studies below. These three examples of unrevised student writings have been subjected to instructional analyses calculated to compel attention to the unrealized possibilities each theme usually represents. The first was written by a freshman, the second by a junior, and the third by a senior, each being the product of an average student for the grade.

I

1. My Public School education ended at P.S. 25. P.S. 25 was
2. built in "1941," so it is a farely new school, and so are the
3. teachers.
4. There are many teachers I liked in P.S. 25 but best of all
5. was Mr. Mann. I liked him because he was informed in the
6. way he did things and made you feel good. He liked to kid
7. around and let the class talk so long as the work was done.
8. I had Mr. Mann for practically everything Math, science,
9. etc. including official class. It was a pretty good set up I had
10. the teacher I liked the most teaching me the subject I liked
11. the most, Math.
12. My favorite program is Dragnet, I like it on both Radio &
13. television. The stories they have are true cases and that's what
14. makes the program interesting.
15. If you read the News or the Mirror you'll see why I like
16. to buy it. You get the news straight. The columns are easy
17. reading & they have a good sport section.

I. Reading for Content, Organization, and Logic

A. What interesting things did you learn about this pupil?
B. Do you agree with his reasons for favoring the TV programs he writes about?
C. What is his reason for liking Mr. Mann?
D. Why did he enjoy some of the other teachers?
E. Why do you think he mentions that P.S. 25 is a new school?
F. What does he mean by getting *the news straight?* by *the columns are easy reading?* by *a good sport section?*
G. This is an autobiography. What do you think of the opening sentence for this theme?
H. Has he used as many paragraphs as he has ideas? How many paragraphs would you have used? Which paragraphs can be consolidated into a single unit?
I. How can he show a possible connection between the third and the fourth paragraphs? between the fourth and fifth?
J. What could have been included in a final sentence to put a finishing touch to this autobiography?

II. Reading to Improve Techniques of Writing

A. *Spelling*
　1. What does he mean by *farely* (line 2)?
　2. How should this word have been written?
　3. Why can there be no such word in the language as *farely?*
　4. How would you rate his spelling ability?
B. *Punctuation*
　1. Why does he place *1941* in quotation marks (line 2)?
　2. Lines 9-11 — Why is additional punctuation needed in this sentence
　3. Line 12 — Why is a comma incorrect here?
C. *Capitalization*
　1. Line 1 — Why should the second and third words be left uncapitalized?
　2. Line 8 — When should the word *math* be capitalized?
　3. Line 12 — Give an example of correct capitalization for *radio.*
　4. Line 15 — Why are the words *News* and *Mirror* capitalized? Use these words in a sentence where no capitalization is required.
D. *Word Usage*
　1. Line 2 — What word should be used for the word *farely?*
　2. Lines 9 and 12 — Why are abbreviations such as *&* and *etc.* not to be used in a composition such as this one?
　3. Line 16 — Why is *buy it* an error in this sentence?
E. *Sentence Structure*
　1. Line 1 — How can the run-on fault in this sentence be corrected?
　2. Line 9 — Why is this a run-on sentence? How can it be improved?
　3. Line 12 — Why does he use a comma in this sentence?
F. *Awkward, Ambiguous, and Redundant Expressions*
　1. Line 2 — Does the phrase, *and so are the teachers,* mean that the teachers are fairly new in the school system, that the teachers were built in 1941, or that the teachers are a fairly new school? How can this thought be clarified?
　2. Line 4 — Was Mr. Mann the best teacher in the school, or was he this pupil's favorite? How can this be more clearly defined?
　3. Line 8 — How can the word order in this sentence be changed to remove the awkwardness of *everything Math, science etc. including official class?*

III. Reading for Exact and Vivid Words

A. Why does the writer use the word *like* seven times in six sentences?
   1. Possible substitutes — admired, respected, enjoyed, desired, fancied, found exciting, favored, most eager to study, preferred, appreciate, control (the class)
   2. Which of these is most appropriate in the sentences where *like* is used?
B. What does the pupil mean by the expression, *informed in the way he does things?*
   1. Possible substitutes — well informed, well prepared, inspiring, stimulating, well qualified, master of his subject
   2. Which of these are not included in the pupil's meanings?
C. When is the news not *straight?*
   1. Possible substitutes — exast, unbiased, accurate, faithfully reported, unerringly reported
   2. Which of these would be suitable for the general tone of this writing?
   3. Why would the last expression be inadvisable here?

II

1.   September 24, 1953
2.   293 Stone Avenue
3.   Brooklyn 12, New York
4. Dear Sister:
5.   I was one of your pupils in the eight grade of Our Lady of
6. Loretto School. I would like to tell you a little about this
7. school so you can tell the students in your room how it really
8. is. Before I came to this school I asked some of my friends
9. who already go their. They said it was the best vocational
10. High School. I didn't believe them until I went there. I like
11. this school very much because of the many things you learn
12. and the way they teach you to become real go machinacs and
13. so many other things. The teachers I like very much because
14. they want to help everyone to go on in life like real workmen
15. and good citizens. The best period I like best is science be-
16. cause it shows us how human people live and plants and
17. animals. The best thing about it is the way our teacher proves
18. these things to us by performing expermants. Now I'll think
19. I will tell you the bad things about this school which I don't
20. like is when we change period we have to go from the first
21. floor to the sixth and the lunchroom is very unserviceing and
22. by the time you get something to eat the bell will ring. But I
23. still like the school very much. Well I guess that's all for
24. now. I will be around to see you soon.
25.   Yours Truly,
                                Victor Gands

I. Reading for Content, Organization, and Logic

A. Why does this student like his school?
B. What conditions does he complain of?
C. The school is a six story building. What impression about the space used does the writer erroneously create?

   D. What could he have done about his grievance? Why is it serious to him?

   E. What other reasons can you give for the writer's opinion of science?

   F. What evidence of courtesy is found in this letter?

   G. Should teachers have other objectives in teaching than those mentioned by this pupil? What might these goals be?

   H. Why is one paragraph insufficient for this letter?

   I. Where would you begin other paragraphs?

   J. Did the pupil fulfil the purpose of his letter?

II. Reading for Improvement of Techniques

   A. *Letter Form*

     1. Heading

       a. Why don't the three lines have the same margin?

       b. Why did he put the date on the first line?

       c. Why should the comma be placed after the zone number?

       d. What corrections are needed in the heading?

     2. Salutation

       a. Why is a colon correct here?

       b. When is a comma to be used after the salutation?

     3. Body — Why is the first word to be indented?

     4. Closing

       a. Why is the placement of the closing incorrect?

       b. Why should the second word be a small letter?

       c. Where should the name appear?

   B. *Spelling* (in the body of the letter)

     1. Line 5 — How is this word (eight) pronounced correctly? How would the correct pronunciation give the correct spelling?

     2. Line 12 — What word did this writer want for *go?*

     3. Line 12 — What should this pupil do if he does not find this word (machinacs) in the dictionary column containing *machine?*

     4. Line 18 — How often has this pupil seen this word (expermants)? What would help him spell it correctly?

     5. Comment on this pupil's spelling ability.

   C. *Punctuation*

     1. Why has this pupil made no real errors in punctuation?

     2. Lines 18-22 — Where would a period be most appropriate here?

     3. Why didn't the writer use that punctuation mark here as he did in all the other thought groups?

   D. *Capitalization*

     1. Why does he capitalize *High School?*

     2. Comment on the writer's knowledge of the use of capitals?

   E. *Word Usage*

     1. Line 5 — What is the difference between *eight* and *eighth?*

     2. Line 9 — Why is this form of the word (their) incorrect in this sentence?

     3. Line 10 — Why does he use the correct form (there) here?

     4. Line 10 — What is the difference in meaning between *went* and *had gone?* Which should the writer have used?

     5. Line 15 — What word might be understood to follow *citizens?* If that word were included how would it affect the use of *like?*

     6. Why doesn't the writer mean to use the word *I'll* in Line 18?

     7. Line 21 — What form of the word is correct?

     8. Line 20 — Why is the form *is* incorrect in this clause?

      9. Line 22 — Under what circumstances could the writer have used the tense *will ring* correctly?

F. *Sentence Structure*

    1. Lines 10-13 — How many reasons are given in this sentence? What methods of correction for this run-on sentence can you suggest?

    2. Lines 18-22 — How many thoughts can be logically separated here? How many times did you have to reread it to determine that number? Why should the writer read it the same number of times?

G. *Awkward, Ambiguous, and Redundant Expressions*

    1. Line 7 — What is the writer referring to in the clause, *how it really is?* What does he mean by this expression? How can it be clarified?

    2. Line 8 — What do you think he wanted to ask his friends? Why should he include this knowledge instead of leaving it to the reader to guess?

    3. Line 10 — Why does the word, *went*, express poorly what the writer wants to say? What does he really wish to write?

    4. Line 12 — What does *they* refer to in this sentence? Why should this be clarified?

    5. Line 13 — Why doesn't he specify the points in the phrase, *so many other things?*

    6. Line 13 — What do you expect to read after an opening like, *The teachers I like very much?* As this sentence is written, which point is emphasized? What is the writer actually concerned with

    7. Line 14 — What does he mean by *go on in life?* What can you suggest to make this expression idiomatic?

    8. Line 15 — Which word is redundant here?

    9. Line 16 — What is wrong with the phrase, *human people?*

    10. Lines 16 and 17 — What point concerning *plants and animals* does the writer wish to make? Why is he unsuccessful in expressing the idea?

    11. Line 17 — To what does *it* refer? Why should this be made clear?

    12. Lines 17 and 18 — What thing is the teacher *proving?* What does the writer mean to say?

    13. Lines 19 and 20 — Why is the expression, *which I don't like*, redundant?

    14. Line 21 — The word, *unserviceing*, is an invention of the writer's. What does he have in mind regarding the lunchroom?

    15. How could the pupil have eliminated some of these faults by himself?

III. Reading for Exact and Vivid Words

A. Lines 6 and 7 — What is the difference between the use of *tell* as an activity of the teacher and *tell* as an activity of the writer?

    1. Possible substitutes — inform, describe, advise, report, explain, mention, acquaint, notify, communicate

    2. Which of these substitutes can be used to replace the *tell* in line 6? which for line 7 *tell?*

    3. Which of these can be used only with the addition of other words to make correct idioms?

B. Line 9 — Why is the word, *said*, a weak expression in this context?

    1. Possible substitutes — claim, advise, declare, maintain, assert, think, recommend, submit, suggest, indicate, intimate, praise, pronounce

    2. Which of these would the pupil use from his own knowledge of the school?

    3. Which of these would a student use if he were uncertain about his school?

      4. Which of the substitutes would be most appropriate for your statement about the school you attend?

C. Line 19 — Why is *bad* too general a term to use about a school?

      1. Possible substitutes — disagreeable, annoying, irritating, displeasing, perplexing, undesirable, unfair, alarming, objectionable, shameful, shocking, disgraceful

      2. Which of these are relevant to the conditions noted by the pupil?

      3. When might you use the word, *perplexing,* to describe a school condition?

      4. What school regulation is *irritating* but not *undesirable?*

      5. Mention some antonyms for these substitutes, and indicate the rules they describe.

D. Line 15 — What conditions make a period a *best* one?

      1. Possible substitutes — favorite, stimulating, exciting, absorbing, interesting, instructive, profitable, enjoyable

      2. How is a *stimulating* period sometimes different from a favorite period?

      3. What does the word *instructive* imply?

      4. Which of these would describe your *best* period?

E. How many words in this letter have two or more syllables?

F. Why should this student be urged to use some of the substitutes suggested above?

III

1.   I Macbeth was once a man of good and God fearing char-
2. acter. I was once a man who knew and felt loyalty. I once had
3. trust and could be trusted without a moment's hesitation. I
4. was a great man who had everything, and more than could be
5. asked of life or wanted from life. I had ambition — yes ambi-
6. tion how such a thing can twist and kill a man.
7.   I do not know when this thing started, I only know it came
8. in controll of my every breath. Perhaps I could have over-
9. thrown it but it was not in the hands of fate but in the hands
10. of the unatural. This destiny was not mine alone — but be-
11. longed to evil.
12.   In achieving my purpose in life, if I may call it that my
13. sense of humanity is progressively dulled — to a point where I
14. know none.
15.   In trying to retain my prrpose in life I became a monster,
16. capable of any blood enormity — and of this I can tell you I
17. did not fall short of.
18.   I am possesed by this ambition and 1 know that eventualy
19. this will cause my mind and soul everlasting damnation.

I. Reading for Content, Logic, and Organization

A. How has this essay captured the spirit of Macbeth, the man?

B. What evidence does the drama supply to justify the statement, *I became a monster?*

C. Why do we pity Macbeth despite his self description?

D. At what point in the drama does Macbeth express fear of *everlasting damnation?*

E. Why doesn't Macbeth act to avoid this horrible future?

F. When might Macbeth have written this confession?

G. Why is there no mention of Lady Macbeth and the witches?

H. At what point in this avowal might these influences have been introduced?

I. Why does the pupil begin a new paragraph in line 15?

J. Point out the effectiveness of the first and last sentences.

K. Where could the writer have introduced a simile or metaphor to invigorate the portrayal?

L. Where could such connectives as *equally important, besides, in addition to,* or *furthermore* be used in this theme?

M. How does the writer, herself, achieve climax in sequence of details?

II. Reading for Improvement of Techniques

A. *Spelling*

1. Line 8 — Why does the writer double the final letter? Would the dictionary help her in this case?

2. Line 8 — When is a hyphen used to separate two combined words? Why might an older dictionary be misleading in such information?

3. Line 10 — Is there a rule for the doubling of letters which would apply here?

4. Line 15 — Why does this (prrpose) appear to be a typing error rather than the writer's mistake in spelling? How could the pupil avoid such faults?

5. Line 18 — Would this writer spell the word (possesed) correctly without the final *ed*?

6. Line 18 — Is there a rule for the doubling of letters which applies to this word (eventualy)?

7. Line 19 — Why didn't the writer use a hyphen for the word *everlasting* or *God fearing*?

B. *Punctuation*

1. Line 1 — Why is punctuation needed before and after *Macbeth*?

2. Lines 5, 10, 13, 16 — Which of these uses of a dash as a punctuation mark is acceptable? When does a pause in a sentence require a dash? What punctuation is useful in each of the cases where a dash is unnecessary?

3. Line 5 — Why is punctuation needed after *yes*?

4. Line 9 — How would a punctuation mark after *it* change the reading of the sentence?

5. Line 12 — What mark is needed after *that*? How would parentheses change that clause?

6. Line 16 — Compare the punctuation in the previous clause (line 12) with *I can tell you.*

C. *Capitalization*

1. Line 1 — Why is *God* capitalized here?

2. Line 19 — What significance would *everlasting damnation* have if the words were capitalized?

D. *Word Usage*

1. Line 10 — Why is *unnatural* a poorly chosen word for this context? What word did the writer have in mind in speaking of the witches? How do these words differ?

2. Line 9 — What is the antecedent for *it*? How can this be clarified?

3. Line 13 — Why is the tense of the verb *is* illogical in this single sentence paragraph?

E. *Awkward, Ambiguous, and Redundant Expressions*

1. Line 3 — Why is the word *trust* unidiomatic here? What word would

be more appropriate? What evidence is there in the drama to prove that Macbeth possessed such a quality?

2. Line 5 — What is the difference between *wanted from life* and *asked of life?*

3. Line 6 — Why would the phrase, *kill and twist a man,* be less effective than *twist and kill a man?*

4. Line 9 — What does the pronoun *it* refer to? Why is *overthrown* inappropriate for this antecedent?

5. Lines 7 and 8 — What is the difference between *took control* and *came in control* in this context?

6. Line 10 — What does the writer mean by *belonged to evil?* How can this be clarified?

7. Line 14 — What is the antecedent for *none?* Why is *know* an inappropriate verb for this object?

8. Line 17 — Why is *fall short of* awkward here? What would be a more fitting verb?

9. Line 17 — Why is the last word on the line redundant?

10. Line 18 — What is the difference between *possessed and obsessed* in this context?

11. Line 16 — What is the antecedent of *this?* What should be added to elucidate the point to be made?

F. *Sentence Structure*

1. Line 1 — Why is the repetition of the phrase, *I was once,* a commendable practice in this paragraph?

2. Lines 3-5 — How can this thought be polished so as to avoid what appears to be a run on sentence?

3. Line 5 — Does the lack of punctuation after *ambition* hinder the smooth reading of this added clause? How can it be reworded to help the reader?

4. Line 9 — Why does the writer use *but* twice? What effect does this have on the structure of the sentence? How can this be corrected?

III. Reading for Exact and Vivid Words

A. Line 4 — What does the writer mean by *great?*

1. Possible substitutes — influential, noble, highly respected, celebrity, magnate, reputable, talented, leader, mighty, eminent, majestic, pillar of the state, paragon, immortal, renowned, esteemed.

2. Which of the above can be substituted as an adjective for *great?*

3. Why is *great man* preferable to any of the substitutes?

4. Which of these words would be descriptive of Macbeth at the beginning of the play?

5. Mention some antonyms of these words applicable to the traits Macbeth revealed toward the close of the drama.

B. Line 8 — Why is *overthrown* poorly chosen to describe the action here?

1. Possible substitutes — conquer, avoid, overcome, surmount, elude, circumvent, check, upset

2. Which of these are not synonyms?

3. Use as many as possible to describe the crimes Macbeth committed.

C. Line 16 — Why is the characterization, *capable of any blood enormity,* an example of well chosen words? How would *bloody* (for *blood*) change that concept?

Point out other examples of felicitous phrases and clauses.

   D. Line 18 — Why is *cause* inadequate to express Macbeth's despair?
      1. Possible substitutes — culminate in, advance, contribute, hasten, intensify
      2. What auxiliary words are necessary to enable these words to function correctly in the sentence?

Benefits of the Method

As can be seen, the questions formulated for each paper are directed toward all the members of a class. Emphasis on thinking in all aspects of composition work is a major aim. Content, organization, and logic receive immediate attention as matters of prime concern while the mechanics of writing take secondary importance. A knowledge of the rules of writing is obtained inductively, whenever possible. The student can see the reason governing the use of a punctuation mark, for example, from the attempt made to read a thought intelligently without such a point of clarification.

It will readily be admitted that immediate results in terms of increased fluency of expression, logical organization, appropriate use of words or correct techniques will not be recorded. However, the pupils who have had the experience of acting as critics have revealed understandings teachers tap but rarely in the daily recitation. Needless to say, the habits, skills, and learnings to be derived from purposeful rereading of the work of others will be much more easily and swiftly attained if this program of writing is initiated early in the writing career of each child. Such evaluative measures as are projected by this method will make lay readers of each of our pupils. Furthermore, we will be able to devote more time to tasks closely related to the development of literature appreciation, responsibilities we tend to neglect in our anxiety to keep up with the mountains of papers which are the affliction of the language arts teacher of today.

For the teacher who likes to instruct the group as he corrects composition weaknesses, Edwin Peterson's "magic lantern" is the answer. Strong verbs, meaningful patterns of structure, various uses of the comma — all these come alive on the background screen as the teacher continues to face his class while correcting, underscoring, and commenting. The author notes that better teacher preparation, more alive response, and better retention of the matter covered are some of the noticeable results of this visual approach to writing.

A MAGIC LANTERN FOR ENGLISH*

EDWIN L. PETERSON

Three years ago, driven to desperation by the poor quality of student writing, the Department of English at the University of Pittsburgh took novel measures to improve the quality of instruction in English composition.

Now that those three years have passed, we want to give other despairing teachers and administrators a message of good tidings, for the counterattack we devised, almost accidentally, has been successful beyond our expectations, even beyond our hopes.

The first step was to arrange our schedules on a team teaching pattern. Two of our most experienced composition teachers conducted large lecture sections that met once a week. These sections then were divided into small workshop sections that met twice a week with young and inexperienced teachers. The young teachers, of course, attended the large lectures, took notes just as the freshmen did, and met once a week with the two experienced teachers in a seminar, where the work of the coming year was laid out. So far there was nothing unusual in the plan.

We soon learned, however, that even an experienced teacher had trouble instructing a class of 300 freshmen and thirty young teachers in required English. Then we discovered that modern teaching miracle, the overhead projector. Immediately, we began to solve problems that we had never been able to solve before — whether in the large class or the small.

When using the overhead projector, the instructor faces his class in a fully lighted room and lays his material on the platform of the projector. As he does so, an image of the material flashes on a ten-foot screen behind the instructor. Let us say that the material is a student theme that the instructor wishes to correct. The theme has already been transferred from the original draft to a transparent acetate sheet. With a grease pencil, the instructor crosses out words on the acetate sheet, inserts commas, replaces bad phrases with good. His pencil marks move boldly across the screen. When he has finished, everyone in the room — not just one student — has profited by the corrections and revisions.

*Edwin L. Peterson, "A Magic Lantern for English," *NEA Journal*, LIII (October 1962), 18-19. Used by permission of Edwin L. Peterson and *NEA Journal*, Mildred S. Fenner, Editor.

Or suppose the instructor wishes to show the importance of the verb in good writing. By the old method he reads his class a passage from William Faulkner, let us say, and asks the students to notice and remember the excellent choice of verbs. The results are, of course, discouraging, for the student is not able to notice the verbs and to remember them from an oral reading. Writing and reading are, in the main, visual experiences. We have to see a sentence, for example, before we can revise it — the adjectives, the phrases, the verbs. Yet in the ordinary class-room it is impossible to do this seeing.

By the new method, the verbs in the Faulkner paragraph can be polarized so that they shine out on the screen in brilliant white light while the other words fade to a dark blue. Then the instructor points out those verbs, one by one, on the screen, where everyone can see them instead of having to take them on faith and vague memory. So effective and self-explanatory is the new method that I honestly believe it can turn a C teacher into a B or an A— teacher.

When the instructor is teaching the structure of the expository paragraph, he shows the paragraph on the screen; then with an overlay he colors the topic sentence red; with another overlay he colors the subtopic sentences green; and with a third overlay he colors the closing sentence red. The class sees the structural pattern taking shape, and the double impact of seeing and hearing gives depth to the learning process. The overhead is, as the *New York Times* has suggested, "a magic lantern" for teaching English.

Even the teaching of punctuation becomes easier and less dull with the overhead projector. Let us say that the instructor is suggesting the wisdom of a comma after an introductory dependent element. On the screen flash the words, "While he was reading the printed page began to blur." More than half the class will misread the sentence and will pause for reconsideration at the word *page*. An orange overlay colors "While he was reading" and identifies it as the dependent element. Then a large red comma appears on the screen after the word *reading*. The comma blinks on and off, on and off.

Experience tells us that the class learns this simple rule of punctuation in about half the time required by the old method. Moreover, the students are interested. Even those in the back row would rather look at the mysteriously blinking comma than at the street outside the window.

The new method saves much class time, too. We prepare our lessons more carefully than before. Because the students learn more quickly, we cover more material in an hour. We no longer waste time fumbling through a stack of books we have brought to class, for the illustrations are on transparencies at our finger tips.

We no longer turn our backs to the students and lose their attention as we write on the old-fashioned blackboard in an illegible script. Instead, we write in our normal handwriting on a sheet of plastic carbon. As we do so, magic white letters march across the black screen, and the students sit entranced at the drama and the mystery of the writing. More important, they remember what the instructor writes, and so do the young teachers.

The drama of the screen has increased the appeal of our Freshman English to the point where ninety-eight percent of the freshmen say that they actually enjoy the course. And we who teach the course know that our students and our intraining teachers are learning more rapidly and more deeply than ever before. We are excited at what seems to be a major breakthrough in the teaching of composition.

If we make the most of this breakthrough, the teaching of composition in the high schools and colleges of America will take, I think, a much needed turn for the better. Already we have made a good start. In the summer of 1962, more than forty colleges and universities participated in our summer institutes in the use of the overhead projector for the teaching of composition.

This participation was made possible through funds granted by the United States Office of Education. In the summer of 1963, we shall have more of these institutes, and we shall open them not only to college teachers but also to high school teachers.

In another practical way we are widening the breakthrough. We are making our carefully planned transparencies available to other colleges — a complete course in college composition, one that has been eminently successful. With the help of high school teachers, we are also preparing a course in high school composition.

With a course content that, over many years, has won an enviable reputation and with a modern technique of presentation that has been wonderfully successful, I feel certain, for the first time in almost four decades of teaching composition, that we have a formula that can enable either high school or college students to write better.

THE TOTAL WRITING PRACTICE: Does the Teacher See All Its Aspects
When Evaluating?

   "Evaluating Expository Writing" by R. Stanley Peterson

   "Evaluating a Theme" from Michigan *Newsletter*

   "Writer's Cramp and Eyestrain — Are They Paying Off?" by Lois V.
   Arnold

The essays in this section relate to all steps involved in the things communicated: the creative process itself, the narrowing of a concept to fit one's purpose,
the communicated "product," and the teacher's evaluation of it.

R. Stanley Peterson's paper centers on analysis of the steps in the student's
thinking prior to outlining and his intention or purpose in relation to the assignment. Organization, coherence, and style come in for their share of criticism
through the sample themes the author uses to demonstrate his plan for improving student writing sans "repression from grades." In his conclusion, Mr. Peterson offers teachers his own system for evaluation, which emphasizes his "constructive aspects" for the teaching of writing.

In the second paper, Lois Arnold outlines implications for definite needs —
improved techniques for motivating writing, inservice aids and teacher courses,
time set aside for private conferences with students — seen from her year's study
of several tenth grade English classes and their multi-evaluated themes.

The case study of a single high school theme by twenty-one college teachers
(mentioned in Mr. Levine's paper above) provides some interesting insights
into college standards "at work." A warning against assigning topics which are
too large in scope, the study also stands as a reproach to evaluations lacking
relevancy and truth.

Given at the Eighth Yale Conference on the Teaching of English in 1962, Mr. Peterson's discussion on grading places the emphasis on how well the writer carries out the intention implicit in the assignment. In the several examples and analyses accompanying his remarks, the author gives particular care to intention, noting that discrepancies in the student's intention and that of the teacher should not necessarily rate his work failure. He favors personal conferences especially for those students who tend to generalize — a habit which, he claims, "no amount of red ink in the margin" will eradicate.

EVALUATING EXPOSITORY WRITING*

R. Stanley Peterson

I had been reading the other night in Frazer's *Golden Bough*, as I sometimes do, when I chanced upon this paragraph concerning contagious magic. "The sympathetic connexion supposed to exist between a man and the weapon which has wounded him is probably founded on the notion that the blood of the weapon continues to feed with the blood in his body. For a like reason the Papuans of Tumleo, an island off New Guinea, are careful to throw into the sea the bloody bandages with which their wounds have been dressed, for they fear that if these rags fell into the hands of an enemy he might injure them magically thereby. Strained and unnatural as this idea may seem to us, it is perhaps less so than the belief that magic sympathy is maintained between a person and his clothes, so that whatever is done to the clothes will be felt by the man himself, even though he may be far away at the time. In the Wotjobaluk tribe of Victoria a wizard would sometimes get hold of a man's opossum rug and roast it slowly in the fire, and as he did so the owner of the rug would fall sick. If the wizard consented to undo the charm, he would give the rug back to the sick man's friends, bidding them put it in water, 'so as to wash the fire out.' When that happened the sufferer would feel a refreshing coolness and probably recover."

Of course I made the inevitable connection. I thought of your students and mine and of the blood letting which our red pencils have caused. From our hands they receive their brain children dripping with gore. Is it any wonder that they shudder and wish to throw the bloody messes into the most convenient trashcan sea? Do they not fear that the bloody bandages may fall into the hands of some college admissions office who is sample hunting? Is it not to be expected that they will resent the injury done to the opossum rug? Would it not be better if the magician consented to undo the charm by removing the offending fire of negative comment so that the sufferer would feel a refreshing coolness and probably recover?

The trouble with grading papers is that the wrong end is most often sought: teachers have to give grades at the end of nine weeks or at the end of the semester — ergo, every composition must have a grade; whereas the end should be

---

*Address presented at the Yale Conference, New Haven, Connecticut, April 13-14, 1962. Used by permission of R. Stanley Peterson.

the improvement of writing. I would substitute some other method than blood letting. I would rub out even the red pencil. I would eliminate the grade. I would —but, as Cummings would say: — listen: there's a hell of a good universe next door; let's go. This is the purpose of the investigation today. What would *I* do about evaluating expository compositions?

I have assembled for you today four themes written by an average class in eleventh grade English. They are not the worst papers one could imagine. They are certainly not the best. They illustrate just about all the important faults of expository writing and at least some of the virtues. I have tampered with the manuscripts somewhat, and I hope you will forgive me. I have removed most of the technical errors of spelling and punctuation. I have done so because I have faith that these are not the kinds of errors you wish to talk about today. I wish to remove the obvious faults and concentrate on some of the factors in writing that are harder to evaluate but which are infinitely more important for the student to learn. For as I see the problem, it is this: the aim in evaluating composition is not an ultimate grade but improved writing.

The Assignment

First, let me explain the assignment. The teacher responsible for this composition problem writes as follows:

Truth Paper

The purpose for giving the assignment of writing on Truth had as many edges as there are to the topic itself. First, since the students had just finished *The Scarlet Letter* and were about to read *The Crucible*, they were in the midst of the issue of truth. The paper would help them to take the issue from the page and into their immediate life. Second, it was an exercise in *writing*. The temptations to verbalize and to ride high in the air and forget that their feet were on solid earth were inherent in the topic. The topic was a test of what they might have learned about solid reasoning and solid exposition.

Before assigning the paper, I gave the students four situations which they might face. These situations involved choices between the truth or a lie.

1) The student was told that in the three months since he received his driver's license, he had maneuvered three minor accidents. His parents warned him that if he had a fourth accident within the next three months, he would lose car privileges for a month. A big weekend was approaching and he needed the car. However, a week before the important weekend, he had backed the car into a pole and dented the bumper. Would he go home and tell his parents about the accident, or would he hope they did not discover it until later?

2) Each boy in the class borrowed one of his father's golf clubs. He did not ask permission to use the club because his parents were away. While playing golf, he broke the club. Would he tell his father immediately, or hope that his father would find it and never suspect him?

Each girl in the class borrowed a pair of her mother's earrings to wear to a dance. She did not ask permission because her mother was away. When she arrived home from the dance, the student discovered that she had lost the earrings. Would she tell her mother when her mother came home or would she remain silent?

3) When writing his library theme, the student copied a passage from a source. He did not give credit for the information. When his teacher asked him whether he had plagiarized on purpose, would he admit the plagiarism or say he forgot?

4) Each student in class started his first job six months ago. During that time he learned that his employer was temperamental. Few jobs were safe if the employer was feeling irritable. One afternoon, the student threw a spitball which ricocheted off the wall and hit the back of his employer's neck. The employer flew into a rage and began an inquisition of each person in the room. No one had seen the student throw the spitball. If he confessed, he would lose his job or the raise in pay that was supposed to come soon. Would he admit his "crime" or keep silent?

After the examples were given, the students were asked to write on the reasons *why* people have valued truth so highly. They were to use the examples to determine their own positions on the question and to keep their ponderings in the realm of their own lives.

Analysis of the Assignment

The instructions to the students, incorporated in the last paragraph of the teacher's statement, were clear. They were to write on the reasons why people have valued truth so highly. They were further warned to use examples from their own experience. The teacher's awareness, then, of the dangers implicit in the type of assignment given is clear. She wanted every student to understand the limitations of his subject, to have his intention clearly in mind, and to avoid the loose verbalizing that such a topic as "Truth" might inspire in adolescent writings.

Four situations were spelled out, which involved incidents that might have happened in the lives of most students. One pertained to driving a car, one to borrowed sports equipment, one to school work, and one to part-time work outside of school. The cautious observer raises only one question: How does the student move from particular incidents to generalizations about *why* people have valued truth so highly? It will be interesting to examine the themes themselves to see whether the assignment (or rather the intention of the assignment) was carried out. If the student departed from the avowed intention of the paper, taking upon himself a different aim, what then? Is he to fail because he did not do what the teacher asked him to do, or is he to be evaluated on his own achievement in terms of his own intention? Our analysis of the individual themes may perhaps clarify this problem.

Truth (A)

Since I was very small I have been taught that truth is a very important part of life. I have been taught that above all truth is right. Never wishing to be at the wrong end of my father's temper I accepted his judgments. It was not until I was about ten or twelve that I began to think and form my own opinion of truth. It was a trip to Canada that started my questioning my father's definition of truth. We were visiting my uncle, who lives in Minnesota, just across the Rainy River from Canada. We took a ferry boat to visit the small village across from my uncle's. My father is always looking for new novelties and came across an extraordinary tie clip which he bought for fifty cents or so. On our trip home we had to pass customs and declare if we had bought anything during our stay. The ferry was just leaving, with an hour wait before the next one. If we declared the tie clip and took the time to pay two or three cents customs duty, we would miss this ferry. My father told us all to be quiet and we didn't declare the clip, but we did make the ferry.

This upset me at the time, I remember, because it was against the principles I had been taught. What was worse, it was my teacher that went against them. That is neither here nor there but it was cause to wonder. I still wonder about truth as it applies to me. Through my childhood I have come to believe that in all situations truth is my goal. I may put it off or slight it a little, but always it's the truth. For example if I broke my father's golf club sometime I wouldn't say anything right away. I would wait until he asked about it or until I thought it was a good time. I would feel it my duty to replace it out of my own earnings.

Why do I try to tell the truth? I do because I let my conscience be my guide. It depends upon the situation as to how much truth I tell. This is like evading one's income tax I suppose and most likely the government will some day catch up with me. Until then I will continue to do as I do, and I do try to be sincere in all I do.

Analysis of Theme A

I should be looking first for acknowledgment of the teacher's intention for the theme — or for the student's alteration of the intention. I do not see how I can avoid looking for one or the other. The progress in the student's thinking seems to run something like this: the student recognizes a time sequence in her moral development — first, authority; second, fear; third, personal judgment. Then follows an incident about the tie clip which raised the doubt. At this point the theme breaks down. The student cannot generalize from the experience and must fall back upon citing the given example about father's golf clubs. Perhaps it is asking too much of a sixteen-year-old to make this subtle decision. I would suggest omitting most of the paragraph, especially sentences 3 and 5 and the final incident about the golf club.

In the last paragraph the student writer stumbles upon a purpose for his theme: "Why do I try to tell the truth?" The student has already tried to answer this question in the first paragraph but now succeeds only in muddying the waters by talking about income tax, which she obviously knows little about. The almost amoral remarks at the end of the theme are due, I suspect, to confusion of aim rather than to an embittered life.

The primary difficulty in this theme is reflected in the title, which does not provide the student with proper direction. If she had said, "Why I Tell the Truth," she would have avoided most of her difficulty, for then she would have known her intention and avoided proliferations. The theme falls apart when "telling the truth" becomes simply a matter of convenience and does not follow from earlier statements.

The only way in which this theme can be evaluated so that it will become a true learning experience for the student is for the teacher to sit down and work through the logical sequence of ideas, elicit proper transition words, phrases, and clauses that will indicate to the student that writing is a sequence and a consequence of idea and example.

There is hope for this student. Her language is better than average; her sentences are generally acceptable; her mechanics are good. What is wrong with her composition, no amount of red ink in the margin is going to improve. I suspect, too, that the assignment was a little difficult for this mind which was too immature to make generalizations, but the validity of the assignment is indicated by the partial success which this student has achieved.

Shall we attempt some kind of evaluation?

Intention . . . Fair

Organization . . . Poor

Language . . . Better than average

Transitions . . . Fair

If a grade has to be given, I suspect that most teachers would give this theme a low C. I would prefer to reserve the grade until the student had rewritten the theme, in which case the grade might conceivably be higher.

Truth (B)

From babyhood we are faced with the problem of telling the truth. At first our parents may use force to instill in us the importance of the truth. When we are young, we tend to make up "stories" to tell in place of what actually happened. Perhaps we can attribute these little "stories" to a child's vivid imagination. However, if a child is not shown that even a little lie is a bad lie, the results may be tragic. Little fibs and white lies lead to big ugly, black lies. For example, if a child is not punished for lying, his conscience probably will not bother him and he will lie as an adolescent or adult. And, if the conscience is not troubled after telling a lie, what is the point in telling the truth? I feel that a person's conscience should be his guide. If a normal person tells a lie, whether it hurts another person or not, his conscience is likely to bother him. This is true especially if the lie hurts someone else. Thus he is faced with a decision. He can either suffer under the power of his conscience and let the lie live, or clear his conscience by letting the truth of the matter be known. However, a person who has been a chronic liar since childhood will probably have no conscience problem because of lies, even though it may hurt others. Similarly, he will lie to protect himself at the cost of others. The point in these examples is simple. Lying is a matter of conscience. Even though liars are despised, the real punishment lies within one's self. Therefore, truth should stem from a sincere desire to be honest with oneself and others at all times.

Analysis of Theme B

The author of Theme B has a facile pen. The paragraph moves swiftly. The transitions, at first glance, seem appropriate. Technically, the theme is faultless — almost. And yet, this is a very poor theme. In the first place, the author does not follow the assignment; he does not discuss the problem of truth.

If you, as teacher, can find it in your heart to be charitable, at least you can expect a clear statement of the writer's own intention. I take his intention to be the origin and development of conscience. If this is true, the student stumbled upon it in the course of his writing. It is not explicitly stated until the last sentence. It is a good sentence, but unfortunately the path to it is cluttered with generalities. As I see this theme, the writer begins with an historical approach describing how the young mind experiments with truth and untruth. It deals with punishment or the tragedy that may spring from a lack of punishment. Logically the theme should then proceed to the development of conscience and conclude with the effect of conscience in the life of the student.

How can this theme be improved? How can it be evaluated? Only through conference with the student, for no amount of writing on the margins can explain to a student what is wrong here. The problem is again one of failure to express an intention. If the student can just decide where he is going, he will have much less trouble than he has had here. Each sentence has to be traced through logically. Each false start must be checked. Each proliferation must be halted. Note how the person changes, for example, ringing all the changes of the personal pronouns, the voices, and the moods.

Comparatively, is this a better theme than Theme A? Frankly, no. I would not like to give it a grade at all until it is made to say something specific about a subject. I would want the student to get off his generalization kick and write what I can feel is his own.

Intention . . . Poor

Organization . . . Poor

Language . . . Good

Reasoning . . . Fair

THE IMPORTANCE OF TRUTH (C)

Every day of our lives a decision of some magnitude must be made by everyone, and it is often when a person finds it hard to tell the truth. The importance of telling the truth cannot always be seen by a person because the long range benefits are constantly being hidden. It is much easier to see the consequences at hand, such as the licking which is to come. The long range benefits are made obscure by fear, and a person does not realize that the physical and mental anguish which is received at the present time because one tells the truth will be much less than the fear compounded in your conscience and your heart afterwards. For a person's own benefits the truth should be told so he can live with himself. The mind is a mighty weapon and when it turns against you it can wreak a violent punishment.

Another reason it is important to tell the truth is that one lie leads to many others. After a person gets away with the first lie, the second lie becomes easier, and the next one easier yet, until they become everyday habits. A person turns to lying as a way of not facing reality, and he always takes the "easy" way out. The "easy" way out, however, does not become easier as one progresses, but it becomes more painful. Pebbles turn to stones and pretty soon a person can become "a nothing" with troubles facing him at every turn. He cannot face life, and his life is worthless because he can do nothing but lie. To do something in life one must, therefore, always tell the truth.

While it would be foolish and idealistic to pretend that truth is all around us we must fight lies to the end. In our newspapers we can see the press misrepresenting statements, and in business we find people who are trying to get ahead in any manner possible. While the truth is not always represented here we must still be true to ourselves and to others. We must try to work toward truth, thereby being a shining light, and we must force truth's virtues into the world with us.

Analysis of Theme C

The author of Theme C is obviously a good student, sensitive to language and to the world around him. He also sees relationships, can argue logically and quite convincingly. He has an occasional lapse in usage, but generally the style is good, though the young man has been frightened at some time or other by a first person pronoun and the trauma has driven him cowering into the passive voice. I am sure that even a short conference could straighten out this major defect of point of view: it shifts from *our* to *a person* to *your* to *one* to *a person* to *one* to *it* to *pebbles* to *he* to *one* — until the poor reader is lost in the confusion and the theme loses vigor. If the first two paragraphs could be rewritten from the original first person point of view, then the last paragraph fits in well and the whole theme will have proper direction and force.

Shall we try to evaluate this theme by means of the categories already set forth?

Intention . . . Good
Organization . . . Good
Language . . . Good
Reasoning . . . Good
Vigor . . . Fair
Content . . . Fair

Most teachers, I think, would be inclined to give this theme a B grade. It has the possibilities of excellence in a good revision using a consistent point of view.

TRUTH (D)

Since man is a superior animal, he is better equipped to make the necessary decisions which will shape his destiny. Every day he is constantly faced with many varying decisions, most of which he can make with a minimum of effort, until he is confronted with a decision involving truth. When he is in such a situation, his natural animal instinct of self-preservation takes over. Due to this instinct, he fears that by telling the truth he will only be exposing himself to criticism and physical punishment, while he believes that by lying, he will be escaping reality; however, in this state of mind he fails to realize that by keeping the truth within his heart, he is actually only subjecting himself to a more severe mental thrashing. I feel that the great authors stress truth because they fully realize that the momentary pains of physical punishment are not nearly as agonizing as the constant throbbing of a guilty conscience.

Now the question arises whether the truth really is as important as the authors make it seem. At first it would appear that the truth is far from important, for when one looks about this society he sees only graft and corruption; however, he must realize that dishonesty is only so prominent because the unusual is more highly publicized than the usual. Actually the truth is very important, not only to the person who uses it as a way to relieve his mental anguish, but also to the person who hears the truth spoken, for one who knows the value of truth is less liable to become a hypocrite himself.

To think that any one person can be completely true is ridiculously idealistic, because no one is perfect; nevertheless, one must remember that when he lies the first person he deceives is himself.

Analysis of Theme D

The author of Theme D tries to answer the assignment. In paragraph 2 the student raises the question of the importance of truth. He recognizes the fact that dishonesty is prevalent in society, but also that it is publicized more than honesty because it is still "news." Two reasons are offered further: the truth prevents mental anguish and hypocrisy. However, since the assignment asked for examples from their own lives, and since no examples are offered in substantiation of the general statements made, the theme must be rated low in content.

The language of the theme is better than average. It has a smooth, convincing flow and is marred by only an occasional incomplete comparison, an inexact conjunction, or a tired transition phrase, but we might wish that all of our students could use language as well as this student.

The chief fault, as I see it, is the inability of the student to follow out the assignment with specific examples that touch his own life. The theme is verbalizing on a rather high level but without much convincing detail. The theme, as a result, lacks vigor.

Intention . . . Fair
Organization . . . Poor
Language . . . Good
Reasoning . . . Fair
Vigor . . . Fair
Content . . . Poor

Would you like to give this theme a C+, hoping that a revision would do something about the weak final paragraph and the paucity of specific examples?

A System of Evaluation

It seems to me that some system of evaluation must be presented to our students other than a single letter grade. I have at various times experimented with different forms. Some years ago, when the General Composition Test was being prepared for the College Entrance Examination Board, a committee worked out a grading scheme that covered the following points: Content, Organization, Reasoning, Mechanics, and Style. A student could make as much as five points in each category, so that a perfect paper gained 25 points. A's, B's, and C's were adjusted to the scale, and an F would come at that spot where incompetency seemed to be evident.

The University of Illinois in its "Standards in Freshman Rhetoric" suggests a nine-point scale with ratings of Poor, Fair, and Good: Content, Originality, Development, Paragraphing, Diction, Grammar, Sentence Structure, Spelling, and Punctuation. This method of evaluating themes has much in its favor, though I sense too great emphasis on mechanics and not enough on the constructive aspects of the teaching of composition.

I shall attempt a third rating scale (and there must be a hundred or more in existence) which I believe can be adapted to secondary school teaching, to individual teachers, and to individual classroom assignments.

INTENTION — Does the student know and demonstrate that he has a purpose in this theme? Does his title suggest his intention? Does he give the reader some indication at the very beginning? Does the theme end with a direct or implied statement of the intention?

CONTENT — Does the student have the required information, recognizable in his use of example, illustration, analogy, comparison or contrast?

REASONING — Is there some flow in idea and argument, made clear and vigorous by proper logic and accurate transitions?

LANGUAGE — Does he use language with precision and clarity, with effectiveness, and some attention to pleasing sound and rhythm? Does he observe standard grammatical forms?

MANUSCRIPT — Is there neatness in format, in margins and signatures and legibility?

EFFORT — Does this theme represent an honest and worthwhile attempt commensurate with the ability of the student?

ACCURACY — Does this theme conform to standard practices in punctuation, spelling, and capitalization?

I have found that in each category it is possible to use the simple device of a plus mark, a check, or a minus sign to indicate the degrees of good, fair, or poor.

The list is perhaps too long; yet it is possible for teachers to vary the number of items used for any individual theme. Exercises might conceivably be given that would involve only Intention, for example, or Content and Language. The teacher can judge. If a total picture is desirable, the teacher could use the entire battery. If there is difficulty in remembering all of the items, he may rearrange them starting with Mechanics, followed by Intention, then Reasoning, etc., so that appropriately he can come up with the acrostic MIRACLE to guide him in the search for the perfect theme.

The themes are now evaluated. Conferences follow. The students know where their weaknesses lie, they know where to concentrate their efforts in making the revisions, and the end result is therefore not a grade to put in the grade book but an improved writing ability to apply to the next writing assignment. Let us hope that the Johnnies and the Janes of America of the future will thus be able to write without repression from grades and that the teachers can have all the time they need to evaluate all themes accurately. It is a consummation devoutly to be wished. And as long as I am being so sanguine, I wish for you no more than a total of eighty students in all of your classes, so that you will be able to do the evaluating I have been talking about today.

Lift up that opossum rug from off the fire and bid your students wash it carefully. Throw away your red pencils and sit down on the log and talk things over. The MIRACLE can happen.

Published in the Newsletter *of the Michigan Council of Teachers of English, this study proves a revealing cross section of the way teachers in the same field vary in their belief about what constitutes good writing. However, as the editor points out, there is evident, also, an astonishing similarity in their outlook when they go about the task of indicating the means which must be taken to revise the theme according to college norms. Evaluators of high school writing should find this study enlightening both from the standpoint of the type of topic assigned plus the writer's handling of it, and the thought provoking comments aimed at the teacher's criticism of it.*

EVALUATING A THEME*

Michigan *Newsletter*

This article, devoted to the evaluating of a single theme, is really a case study in the philosophy of composition and of the teaching of composition. The original article contained twenty-five separate teacher responses to this theme. We have selected one evaluation by a high school teacher and fifteen by college teachers.

Steps — and cautions: (1) Read the teacher's letter. Notice her questions: they shaped many of the responses. (2) Read the theme and the teacher's marginal comments. (3) The evaluations by the college teachers are a demonstration of the "college standard" at work. Unrehearsed, with quirks of personality showing through the chinks, they agree most surprisingly on the steps that should be taken to make the essay a creditable college freshman performance.

(4) Warning: Though some of the comments seem to be directed to the writer of the theme, surely these teachers sent in for publication to fellow teachers something other (and *more*) than they would have scrawled on the theme had it turned up in their own classes. (5) Some responses have been drastically cut and edited; do not judge persons or schools by what is printed here.

Dear Editor:

 May I make a request? I am enclosing a theme written by a good student, not a superior one, a high school junior. Would any instructor of freshman composition have time to evaluate this theme and also my criticism of it?

 This theme is of interest to me because the writer followed the requirement of the assignment exactly — to list several questions on a subject, discuss them, plan an introduction and a closing. (The class after studying *Reader's Digest* articles decided introductions should contain action.)

 If this theme were the work of a freshman, what would your criticisms be? What is good about it? What is poor? What grade would it receive? What is your opinion of the assignment? Would themes about personal experiences or descriptions be better preparation?

 Are too many sentence errors ignored in my marking the theme? Or do you consider them of less importance than the expression of ideas?

Very truly yours,
Louise Fitzgerald

---

*From Michigan Council of Teachers of English, *Newsletter*, V (Spring 1958). Used by permission of A. K. Stevens, Editor.

L.   HOW CAN ACCIDENTS BE PREVENTED

Outline

I.   Should driver's education be made compulsory?

II. Should the age limit be changed from sixteen to eighteen years of age?

Thoughtful and well-organized

III. Are Hot-Rod organizations of any value to the community?

IV. Should there be a limit on the horsepower of a car?

One day after school last year as Leonard and I were rounding the corner at home, going about 40 m.p.h., our car suddenly hit loose gravel

An excellent introduction

that had been pushed up on the pavement and the car suddenly went into one complete spin. The next thing we knew we were in the ditch. No cuts, bruises, or wrecked car but it did make me think what the consequences could have been, and one of the reasons why it would be to everybody's advantage to have compulsory driver's education. If more people were taught

Use less *for quantities that are measured. Use* fewer *for quantities that can be counted.*

the dangers of driving and the correct way to drive, there would undoubtedl; be less accidents.

The age limit in Indiana is sixteen. In some of the other states the legal driving age limit is eighteen. There was considerable debate at the last meeting of the Indiana Legislature on this subject. A bill was introduced to change the age limit from sixteen to eighteen; however, it was not passed. In my opinion a change in the law to include at least one year of driver's education would be of benefit. Then issue license at the age of seventeen.

Do Hot-Rod organizations and driver's education have anything in

What is the subject of this sentence?

common? Yes, reports N.H.R.A., there are many new clubs being started all over the country, their goal, safe driving. They believe that if they can keep Hot-Rod drivers on the designated drag-strips, and off the public streets and highways, they will be doing the public a great favor.

Each year the horse power ratings of the new cars has been steadily increasing. The cars are going faster every year. They have done little toward the braking system and steering, the two most important functions. Also they have not been able to change the people to make their minds react quicker.

a good ending!

There is much publicity on the subject of safe driving: however people seem to take the attitude that it won't happen to me and thousands continue to be killed unnecessarily year after year. Why don't people "wise-up"?

End

(What happened to the question mark?) This theme poses for me at least the old question of whether composition can be taught at all. Certainly we can't teach anyone to write until we show him how to develop a series of ideas in logical order, each one with some thoroughness.

Composition is nothing but sound sense. Dr. C. D. Thorpe once ventured the opinion that it is perfectly possible to have good organization of even the simplest idea, but good organization depends on clear thinking, not tricks. The outline which this teacher has called "thoughtful and well-organized" is not an outline at all; it is merely a succession of four loosely related sentences, any one of which might provide material for a sound composition four times the length of the one presented.

I am troubled by the thought that the mere formality of writing something which passes for an outline seems to have satisfied this teacher. An outline may have value if it outlines, that is, if it presents to the student in vivid form those steps which he should be preparing to take. An outline which serves little or no purpose has little or no value. What is more (and again I am troubled by the reliance on formalism), whatever wisdom one may gain from the *Reader's Digest*, it is about as silly to say that all introductions should contain action as it would be to say that all football games ought to start with a forward pass. The nature of the situation will decide procedure.

The writer of the composition in question errs largely in his failure to relate what may well be admirable points to the essential structure of his argument. It is possible that the driver in the first paragraph might have learned enough in driver education so that he would have refrained from driving forty miles per hour on loose gravel, but in spite of the wisdom that seemed to flow down on him the second he landed in the ditch, one doubts it. One doesn't develop wisdom merely by "taking a course," and he already seemed to know wise procedure. It seems to me that the illustration is piously forced, probably to please teacher.

The fuzzy thinking continues in the next paragraph; there is a complete lack of evidence for or against any age change in licensing. There is merely an assumption, unsupported, that age breeds wisdom, and then a gesture of compromise, all unreasoned.

Paragraph three moves fuzzily onward. The N.H.R.A. (whatever that is) shares with "driver education" (courses in driver education?) a great affection for safe driving. No discussion of hot-rodding adds to our knowledge; as a matter of fact, the timid phrase at the conclusion makes us think of the whole matter as a nuisance rather than a danger.

The fourth paragraph is a garbled and somewhat inaccurate discussion of horse power. No attempt is made to present any justification for the powerful engine, or even any reason for it. The indefinite "they" have, contrary to the opinion expressed, done much to improve braking and steering. A rebuttal to all manufacturers' arguments has been relegated to the final sentence, and even this is inaccurate, since the human "mind" is only one area of human equipment which seems unable to stand up in a speedier world.

The final paragraph is a flat summation which despite its pseudohumorous rhetorical question does not, as I see it, constitute a "good ending."

I'd have to "fail" the paper if it appeared in my class. It would be an unkindness to any student to pass him and to create in him any feeling that work so badly organized, so poorly executed, had any merit. I would have the student in to discover why he wanted to write on a subject so large concerning which he knew so little. If he persisted in his desire to write on this matter I would take time to explore it with him, substituting divisions and subdivisions which actually came out of his own convictions and experiences. I might or might not ask for an outline, depending on whether I thought such a device would be useful.

If there had to be a composition on this wide subject, I would look for far more solid structure in the very first revision. I would insist that each paragraph be properly developed, that facts be stated clearly, that evidence be presented for all statements.

In one of the later revisions (and this student would need quite a few), I would take care of whatever rough language habits had not already been put to order. The language patterns look to me as if they might straighten themselves out once the student knew what he was talking about.

I pass over the teacher's comments. In a spirit of understatement I can only say that were I the student I would not have found them helpful.

—Carl G. Wonnberger, Cranbrook School

II.

General comments: I find your theme dull. Be more vivid, specific, realistic. Increase reader interest. Don't go to the library and copy out pp. of half-digested facts; but ① tell more of what you know + then ② see what ½ doz. authorities say. Your theme needs guts. I'm not persuaded or convinced.

Reread your paper. Ask yourself more questions: "Have the states based their laws on fact, intuition, tradition? Why wasn't the 2nd. leg. bill passed?" Why is 18 the age? etc. etc.

How Can Accidents Be Prevented ?   Subject too, too big!!!

Tho' too big. subj. is worthy

Outline of thought

Why put this here? Attach your outline to your theme.

I. Should driver's education be made compulsory?

outline deadly here

II. Should the age limit be changed from sixteen to eighteen years of age?

III. Are Hot-Rod organizations of any value to the community?

IV. Should there be a limit on the horse-power of a car?

Your theme needs guts. See what Cornell has found on subject.

One day after school last year as Leonard and I were rounding the corner

I get no clear image here. Be specific.

at home, going about 40 m.p.h., our car suddenly hit loose gravel that had

get a better verb!

been pushed up on the pavement, and the car suddenly (went) into one complete

spin. The next thing we knew we were in the ditch. No cuts, bruises, or

work these opening 2 sentences into something more dramatic.

too tame →

wrecked car but it did make me think what the consequences could have been,

You're in the ditch! How can you think so soon?

and one of the reasons why it would be to everybody's advantage to have com-

pulsory driver's education. If more people were taught the dangers of

See Bergen + Cornelia Evans' Dict. of Contemp. American Usage.

driving and the correct way to drive, there would undoubtedly be (less) accidents.

Transition? for what?

The age limit in Indiana is sixteen. In some of the other states the legal

awk)

when? Be specific. Pin it down

driving age limit is eighteen. There was considerable debate at the last

Though a

meeting of the Indiana Legislature on this subject. A bill was introduced to

change the age limit from sixteen to eighteen, however it was not passed. In

my opinion a change in the law to include at least one year of driver's edu-

You shift the subj. here →

cation would be of benefit. Then issue license at the age of seventeen.

In here, find out what a national authority says about it. Why do you think so?

Why caps?

Do Hot-Rod organizations and driver's education have anything in common?

Explain abbrev.

According to

Yes, reports N.H.R.A., there are many new clubs being started all over the

whose is

country, their goal safe driving. They believe that if they can keep Hot-Rod

drivers on the designated drag-strips and off the public streets and highways,

Indeed they will! But has this belief borne fruit? What's happened? You leave us in the lurch!

they will be doing the public a great favor.

from what to what, e.g.?

Each year the horse-power ratings of the new cars has been steadily in-

who?

not too accurate word choice

creasing. The cars are going faster every year. (They) have done little to-

right word?

ward the braking system and steering, the two most important (functions).

Are braking system and steering parallel?

Also they have not been able to change the people to make their minds react

quicker. *Why?*

There is much publicity on the subject of safe driving; however people

couldn't

seem to take the attitude that "It won't happen to me," and thousands continue to

Yes, why don't they? what do psychologists say?

be killed unnecessarily year after year. Why don't people wise up ?

This almost sounds like the same 1000's were being re-killed.

—End

Benjamin B. Hickok,

Michigan State University

III.

Outline

I.   Should driver's education be made compulsory?

Thoughtful and well-organized

II.   Should the age limit be changed from sixteen to eighteen years of age?

III.   Are Hot-Rod organizations of any value to the community?

IV.   Should there be a limit on the horse-power of a car?

An excellent introduction

One day after school last year as Leonard and I were rounding the corner at home, going about 40 m.p.h., our car suddenly hit loose gravel that had been pushed up on the pavement and ~~the car~~ suddenly went into one complete spin. The next thing we knew ~~we were~~ in the ditch. No cuts, bruises, or wrecked car but it did make me think what the consequences could have been, and one of the reasons why it would be to everybody's advantage to have compulsory driver's ~~education.~~ If more people were taught the dangers of driving and the correct way to drive, there would undoubtedly be less accidents.   *pc.*   *coh.*

Use less for quantities that are measured. Use fewer for quantities that can be counted.

pc

The age limit in Indiana is sixteen. In some of the other states the legal driving age limit is eighteen. There was considerable debate at the last meeting of the Indiana Legislature on this subject. A bill was introduced to change the age limit from sixteen to eighteen; however it was not passed. In my opinion a change in the law to include at least one year of driver's education would be of benefit. Then issue license at the age of seventeen.

What is the subject of this sentence?

Do Hot-Rod organizations and driver's education have anything in common? Yes, reports N.H.R.A., there are many new clubs being started all over the country, their goal, safe driving. They believe that if they can keep Hot-Rod drivers on the designated drag-strips, and off the public streets and highways, they will be doing the public a great favor. *accident connection only implied*

who?

Each year the horse power ratings of the new cars (has) been steadily increasing. The cars are going faster every year. (They) have done little toward the braking system and steering, the two most important functions. Also they have not been able to change the people to make their minds react quicker. *idiom*

A good ending

pc.

There is much publicity on the subject of safe driving: *what?* however people seem to take the attitude that (it won't happen to me) and thousands continue to be killed unnecessarily year after year. Why don't people "wise-up"?

Different tone

End

Dear Professor Stevens,

Never having taught an eleventh grade class, I find it difficult to imagine what I would give such a paper (in the way of a grade) and whether or not the assignment should have been given. If the paper is typical of the writing of high school juniors, I *suspect* that I would have my students work on paragraphs somewhat more intensively before attempting any more "long" efforts.

If this paper were submitted to me in about the middle of the first semester of our English 1 course (college freshman level), I would probably give it an F. The chief reasons for the failing grade are poor paragraph development, lack of unity within several of the paragraphs, and failure to integrate the five paragraphs into a coherent whole. The paper is more a series of underdeveloped paragraphs than a tightly knit exposition on "How Accidents Can Be Prevented." There are other problems, some of which I have checked.

It is quite unlikely that I would make all of the marks and comments that I have included here on the student's paper. I have made a variety of comments to suggest to the teacher some of the comments which she might have made. Some of these should probably take priority over the *fewer-less* distinction.

— The construction and meaning after *think* are not clear.

— Suddenly this Intro. ceases to be an Intro. and gives Roman division I a glancing blow.

— There is *no* transition from ¶ 1 to ¶ 2. ¶ 2 seems to develop division II, but reader finds himself back in the division I discussion.

— Transition to ¶ 3 a bit better. You ought to write out full name of an organization before you refer to it by initials only.

— The question posed in division III is not answered in this ¶. New and irrelevant materials have been introduced

Eugene F. Grewe
University of Detroit

IV. What is and is not good about the paper? Since the student followed the teacher's directive, that, in my opinion, is what is good about the paper. The student did have an introduction, a good one; he did have a conclusion, not so good; he did raise several questions. He did not, however, discuss these questions; he did very little beyond stating them. The obvious weakness of the paper, as I see it, is that the student has done too little with too much. Any one of the four questions he raises, properly developed, would have been a sufficiently large topic for a theme of this length. For example, the last sentence in paragraph one states a point of view, a belief of the writer's which we as readers are asked to accept on the basis of the single experience he mentions. As a reader, I do not accept the single instance as a sufficient basis for my believing, although I recognize the plausibility of his view. I expect the writer to provide me with a basis of belief in the next two or three paragraphs. Instead of fulfilling my expectations, he pulls a fast switch. What we are concerned with here then is the old principle of developing an idea fully enough. If that had been done, perhaps the paper would have had a real unity as distinguished from the superficial unity it now has. Since Miss Fitzgerald says, however, that the student did what she asked him to do, she may not have stressed the importance of discussing the questions and she may have considered the discussion adequate. I would not consider it adequate for a college freshman.

What is my opinion of the assignment? It is a legitimate one. I see no reason why it has to be ranked as better or not as good as an assignment in description or personal experience. These three types simply aim at different things. If I must rank them, I would be inclined to place the type here represented as first because it affords a better opportunity for critically examining and, I hope, training the thought process.

Are too many sentence errors ignored? Are they of less importance than the expression of ideas? When the errors interfere with the expression, thy are exceedingly important. In this paper they do not. To me it is a matter of putting first things first. This student needs most to learn to develop ideas fully. Then his sensitivity to the niceties may be cultivated. Miss Fitzgerald has exercised good judgment, it seems to me, by not directing the student's attention to what must be of minor importance at this stage of his development. On the other hand, failure to show the student what is the fundamental weakness of the paper is to leave him in a fool's paradise. (Such a statement assumes, of course, that I know what the fundamental weakness is. The assumption may not be warranted.)

What grade would I give the theme? If I were in a charitable mood (an affliction from which I occasionally suffer), the student would be given a C. If I were suspicious that I had been derelict in my duties (here the other student's themes would tell a story), the student would be entitled to his C. If I were confident that the instruction had been what it should be and if I were in a mood to impartially dispense justice, cost what anguish it may, this paper would receive a D, because reading this is like being invited to a steak dinner only to discover the hostess has provided all the trimmings but no steak!

—Nora Landmark, Michigan State University

V. Ought not each paragraph come back to the main point? Each paragraph here refers only generally to the main issue, but we need more than this general reference.

A sentence in Paragraph One tells us that it is necessary to have compulsory driver's education. This strikes me as the "main point." But the title and the essay are about the *how* of preventing accidents.

Grade: C marks this as the work of an average student; there is nothing here above the average.

—Sister Robert Louise, O.P.; Siena Heights College

VI. Assignments such as this seem to lead the student toward one of the great weaknesses I find among my freshmen writers. The weakness may be simply stated: insufficient development of an inadequately limited idea.

The assignment was to "List several questions on a subject . . .," and the student has achieved the assignment. Yet, I question whether this is good writing; and I wonder if one source of the difficulty does not arise from the assignment itself. It seems admirably suited to the writing of a series of paragraphs, but not to the writing of a "good" theme.

I think this writer needs a specific purpose that will narrow and direct his aim. If he will narrow his purpose to the question: How can (automobile) accidents be prevented? he may have a clearer view of his task. In such a case he would need to revise his outline. Point I would seem appropriate; point II would require some revision, and points III and IV would be revised to fit the purpose or they would be discarded. The conclusion should be revised to tie the supporting materials and purpose together. The assignment would be even better if the writer were forced to narrow his purpose to securing the belief that driver education should be compulsory. This idea is inherent in the first illustration. If such a purpose were stated clearly, the subject would be *limited* and *directed*. It is this lack of limitation and direction that weakens the sample theme. Now if we can force this student to select such a specific purpose (and if he is a good student) he should easily recognize that he will have to discard all of the other material in his outline. He must then gather material that will effectively develop or support his idea. He will not be able to wander widely over God's green earth taking *any* question relative to a subject, but he will select those questions or materials that directly support his limited specific purpose. Then he should produce a unified and coherent piece of writing that would be worthy of being called a "theme."

I would insist that a college student *narrow* his subject, *direct* his aim, and develop that specific purpose adequately. I would require a rewrite of this paper before awarding a grade to a freshman writer.

—Clyde W. Dow, Michigan State University

VII. The tacking on of an introduction and a conclusion to the brief discussion of four separate problems connected with automobile accidents makes the paper an extremely artificial exercise. The unity of the paper is destroyed because the student has no adequate idea of what he is up to when he starts writing. . . . Grade: C.

—C. Merton Babcock, Michigan State University

VIII. I agree with the marginal comments which tell the writer that he has a good beginning and ending. I do not agree that the preliminary questions represent any kind of organization. I do not agree that *less* and *fewer* deserve comment (point made by Evans and Evans in their recent *Dictionary of Contemporary American Usage*). I do not agree that the structure of the last sentence in paragraph two is unacceptable.

—Ben Strandness, Michigan State University

IX. Grade: I would grade this paper D; if it were written toward the end of the first semester it would probably be graded E.

Comment: 1. The paper has certain good features: it is relatively free from mechanical errors; the writer attempts to organize his ideas; it is relatively objective; it includes some detail; the writer's command of sentences is usually good, and he is on his way to a plainspoken, straightforward style.

2. Although it is somewhat mechanical, the assignment is all right because it attempts to stimulate organization of a paper on a principle which is not chronological or biographical. It is desirable to encourage students to use personal experience and their reflections on it in their papers within a more objective organization.

3. Sentence errors are not more important than the expression of ideas, but the expression of ideas will probably not be very good until sentences and paragraphs are mastered.

4. One of the main defects of this paper is that there is only a very general connection between the ideas expressed. The writer has not thought through (nor has he expressed by transitions) the relation of these ideas to the announced topic. The result is that the paper is a collection of assertions and not a coherent argument. The ending is weak because it is so general and unrelated to the rest of the paper.

—W. R. Steinhoff, University of Michigan

X. I am impressed with the ease of expression and the sophistication of vocabulary shown by this high school junior. Many college freshmen do not write at this level. However, I would give it only a C.

I disagree with the instructor's comment on the outline portion of the paper; I do not think the topics are "well organized." They are separate questions with only automobile driving as a common subject; each one could be discussed in such detail as to provide material for an entire theme. . . .

I would not accept "Why don't people 'wise up'?" as an adequate intellectual response to the topics of driver education, age limits for driver's licenses, and the challenge of increased horse power in modern automobiles.

The instructor should be complimented on her ingenious use of the *Newsletter*. It offers hope that in a few years freshman English instructors are going to be blessed with students who can express themselves.

—R. Barrett, University of Michigan

XI. This assignment is good in that it asks the student to deal with ideas, drawing upon his own experience and knowledge, rather than merely to present personal experience in a strictly narrative form. I think, however, that the assignment might be focused somewhat more carefully, and the student asked not only to "discuss" several questions on a subject, but to show the relationship between these questions as well.

The corrections seem appropriate — enough attention has been given to the mechanics of the paper, which, in general, present no serious problem. I think it might be desirable, however, to point out to the student the need for tying the different parts of the paper together more closely. Paragraphs 2, 3, and 4 each suggest a topic for a separate theme, and though they are related to the main topic (i.e., "driver education"), this relationship is not demonstrated with sufficient explicitness. More care with transitions would help to solve this problem. For example, the fourth paragraph might be introduced with an explicit statement of the idea that the increase in horse power ratings has made driver education even more necessary than it was before — and then this paragraph might conceivably become paragraph 2 so that the student demonstrated the seriousness of the situation before going on to suggest solutions. The conclusion, likewise, though good in itself, does not tie all of the ideas of the paper together and seems more like the conclusion for another paper. Grade: D.

—Alan B. Howes, University of Michigan

XII. I dislike the influence of the *Reader's Digest*. One oughtn't try its peppy, memorandum-like style until one can write acceptable English prose. The *Digest* style may be the cause of the transition difficulties. The *Digest* does condense after all.

As for preparation for college, I think the students should be told more or less what to write. This leaves the teacher free to see that the assignment is written properly. In high school, accurate writing of standard English is more important than the expression of ideas.

As a freshman theme, I would give this a C or a C—.

—L. H. Barber, University of Michigan

XIII. If this were a freshman theme, I would grade it D, mainly because it lacks cohesion. A topic is "covered," but it is not developed. Transitions are wanting between paragraphs, and order is needed *within* paragraphs.

The conclusion seems especially weak — the expression of a vague wish that "other people" should reform. Only the first paragraph reveals some *interest* on the writer's part. Probably the assignment was a rather artificial one, and on a journalistically hackneyed topic.

—A. J. Carr, University of Michigan

XIV. The faults are at least partly the result of the assignment. In a paper of this length, the student cannot reasonably be expected to deal adequately with more than one aspect of the topic. To ask him to discuss "several questions" on a topic is to invite problems with thesis and organization. Any one of this student's four questions could have been developed into an excellent short paper.

As to mechanics, I definitely do not consider them "of less importance than the expression of ideas," and this theme contains a number of errors which I would have marked. Calling the student's attention to his errors is the only way I know of getting him to correct them; and if he is going to write acceptably, correct them he must. Grade: C—, possibly lower.

—Lidie McKinney, University of Michigan

XV. The theme lacks coherence, although this may be mainly the fault of the assignment. The student has followed instructions exactly, and the result is disorganization. Any one of these four questions could be the topic of a short theme. Together, they add up to nothing, and the introduction and conclusion are simply tacked on. High school students should be encouraged to develop a single idea consistently and logically.

The teacher's comments, when they aren't mistaken, are concerned with trivialities. Grade: E.

—Worth Harder, Wayne State University

XVI. The chief defect of this paper is that none of its paragraphs is developed to a point that would demonstrate its relevance to the other paragraphs and to the thesis. . . .

A second and still important defect is an inability to give each sentence its own unity and structure. . . .

There are other, less significant defects in phrasing, punctuation, etc., but to list them all would be to confuse the student. If this paper is typical of his work, he has enough to do already. Grade: E.

Leo Stoller, Wayne State University

Miss Arnold describes her lengthy and intensive research into the effects of various types of writing practice and teacher evaluation. The study, designed to include eight tenth grade classes in Florida schools, was carried on over a one-year period.

In two of these groups, compositions received moderate evaluation, one group writing frequently, the other, seldom.

In the third and fourth groups, compositions received intensive evaluation, one group writing as frequently as four times a week, the other writing only three 250 word themes a semester.

Testing programs in May of that year revealed "no differences in group performance resulting from either frequent practice or intensive evaluation." The author concludes that

1. *Intensive evaluation is seemingly no more effective than moderate evaluation in improving the quality of written composition.*
2. *Frequent writing practice does not in itself improve writing.*
3. *There is no evidence that any one combination of frequency of writing and teacher evaluation is more effective than another.*
4. *Frequent writing and intensive evaluation are no more effective for one ability level than are infrequent writing and moderate evaluation.*

The remainder of her article follows.

WRITER'S CRAMP AND EYESTRAIN— ARE THEY PAYING OFF?*

Lois V. Arnold

Just what do these findings imply for the classroom teacher or for the school administrator? Since these conclusions are somewhat contrary to assumptions long accepted as basic to composition instruction, it is important to consider all aspects of the teaching of writing. The person who makes quick judgments will conclude that this study suggests only less writing and less grading. Such is not the case at all. The results of this study, which shows no differences in student performance whether there was frequent or infrequent writing or intensive or moderate evaluation, hold definite implications for the English classroom.

First, there should be careful consideration given to that kind of evaluation which is actually helpful to students. Perhaps the laborious marking of papers, the writing of detailed comments, and the requiring of revisions and corrections represent misdirected effort which might better be spent by the teacher and student in frequent conferences. Those variables such as the conference technique, use of the lay reader, tape recorded evaluations by the teacher, or group discussions were not part of this research study and merit much consideration.

*From Lois V. Arnold, "Writer's Cramp and Eyestrain—Are They Paying Off?" *English Journal*, LII (January 1964), 10-15. Used by permission of Lois V. Arnold.

Second, attention should be directed to those factors constituting the total writing practice. Just what is the relationship between reading and writing? Between thinking and writing? Motivational techniques as such were not considered main effects in this study, but the findings indicate that every teacher of English needs a better understanding of why students write.

A third emphasis should be directed toward preparing teachers of English more adequately for the teaching of composition. While this calls for research studies, an immediate and practical approach could be made through the provision of inservice programs such as workshops, institutes, or group study. College and state certification departments should require advanced courses in composition of prospective teachers of English. When informal surveys indicate that the teaching of composition is one of the areas in which teachers of English feel most inadequate, it would seem that extension courses might be provided teachers already in the field.

Following closely these suggestions for improving teacher preparation would be a fourth emphasis — that of providing teachers with adequate time. Perhaps the schedule-harassed administrator would retort, "But if frequent writing and intensive evaluation are no more effective, why should the English teacher have a lighter load?" Time formerly considered as dedicated to the grading process might then be redirected toward planning for instruction, for conferring with students, and for evaluating progress. Perhaps the teacher of English who reads widely and writes effectively could become a dynamic factor in this teaching of writing.

Finally, attention should be directed to all the writing done by students. This would include written expression done in addition to that in English classes. Is there consensus among faculty members on what constitutes good writing? Is there a need for a faculty-wide study of writing techniques and evaluation? Perhaps the student, tossed as he is on the winds of disagreement, would write more effectively if more of his teachers understood just what the total writing process is — from the moment that the student conceives an idea to the time that he and the teacher consider the written communication of that idea. . . .

In summary, then, it must not be assumed that frequent writing practice and intensive teacher evaluation result in improved written expression. Teachers and administrators would do well to work toward a more thorough understanding of what written composition actually is, what prompts students to write, and what methods of evaluation are most effective. Whether organized research is being done or not, it is only when there is understanding of the total writing process that real progress will be noted.

COMMUNICATION: How Do We Measure Its Success or Failure?

Junior High Level

Senior High Level

The final section of the bulletin contains a variety of types of themes plus standards for evaluating them.

In some instances, comments and criticisms are those of an individual evaluator; in others, they are the pooled findings of a large group of critics drawn from high schools and colleges. Comments to teachers accompany many of the "readings." Some of the remarks addressed to teachers refer to the dangers of assigning certain types of topics; others point up specific means for helping the student-author. Where assigned topics are not stated, criticism grows from the nature of the theme as a whole, thus assisting even the inexperienced teacher to define the success or failure of any theme.

The last paper — a kind of "epilogue" to the bulletin as a whole — indicates logical and specific measures for insuring failure in writing. While accentuating the negative, however, each directive indicates the most important *positive* means for achieving success in written composition. It serves, also, as a summary statement of what to look for when evaluating students' themes.

Junior High Level

These papers are drawn from junior high school classes.
Reasons for the success or failure of each theme are carefully
delineated. In some cases, what is called for by the assigned
topic is not clearly stated; in other cases, vagueness stems from
the student's lack of purpose.

SUGGESTIONS FOR EVALUATING
JUNIOR HIGH SCHOOL WRITING°

Lois M. Grose
Dorothy Miller
Erwin R. Steinberg

Grade 7   Average

Title ?
better what?

I think that dogs are better than cats. Dogs are much better watchers

Can you find a better word than small? because they can bark when they hear a noise and cats have only a (small)

"meow🡒 A cat's scratch on a small child is no fun, for it can bring in-

fection. A dog can run around and wrestle with children and not hurt them.

all you mean is " A dog is cleaner than a cat." Why not say it?

The cleanliness of a dog is much better than that of a cat. (Dogs can

to go

You have two sentences here.
Do you see them ?
be trained to bark when they want out, (even) some people have a little swing-

? ⌐
ing door🡒 so they can go out themselves.) Cats sometimes have a box in a

People go out through a little swinging door? That's what you say.
sp.
room that no one uses to often, but even then it will smell sometimes.

The box or the room ?
Something went wrong here.

In a house where (is) blind people a dog can be a great help. A "seeing

eye" dog helping the blind from room to room is wonderful. (It) makes the
"Blind people is"? Can you fix it ?

blind person's life less dangerous, because if the blind person is by him-

self, he is likely to bump into something and get hurt. *What? The dog? Helping the blind?*

To the Student

You have a lot of good detail. It is hard, however, to tell whether it is all related to your topic. If your title were "Dogs as Pets," your last paragraph would
not fit. If, on the other hand, your title were "I'd Rather Have a Dog than a Cat,"
it would. Do you see now why a title is important?

A concluding sentence which tied everything together would have helped.

*From a publication of the Association of English Teachers of Western Pennsylvania (Cham-
paign, Ill.: National Council of Teachers of English) pp. 20-23, 28-30. Used by permission
of Lois M. Grose, Chairman.

A better way to organize this paper would be to put all the information about dogs in one paragraph and all the information about cats in another. In that way you wouldn't have to jump from one to the other the way you do in your first paragraph.

To THE TEACHER

In making comparisons, inexperienced writers often attempt the point for point analysis that this student did. Such an attempt, however, generally fails for several reasons. First, such a method of comparison requires facility in making transitions, a rather sophisticated matter for most junior high school students. Thus, the first paragraph should have read:

> I think that dogs make better pets than cats and are more useful. *For example,* dogs are better watchers because they can bark loudly when they hear a noise. Cats can only "meow" weakly. *And* a dog can run around or wrestle with children and not hurt them. *But* a cat often scratches children and not only hurts them but causes infection.

Note also that this sort of comparison requires constant parallelism, which is also difficult.

The final difficulty with this sort of comparison is that the writer almost invariably runs out of points of exact comparison but finds himself with points on one or both sides that should be considered. He is left, then, with several possibilities, none of which is very good: to continue the alternation, even though the paired items are not really comparisons; to drop the alternation and conclude with a short paragraph about each (i.e., to change the basic pattern at the conclusion, generally with the weakest points of the argument in the concluding paragraphs); or, as the student did here, to run out of material for one side of the comparison and simply drop it.

The third sentence in the first paragraph and the last sentence in the second paragraph also indicate that the student can't always maintain the focus that she should. They point away from the comparisons that they should make instead of toward them.

Grade 7   **Good**

In <u>Memory</u> of <u>Topsy</u> } *You don't have to underline a title.*

With her black hair and brown eyes, long ears, and short tail she

sp.
was <u>irresistable</u>. She wasn<u>'</u>t too fat <u>nor</u> too thin and she loved to be   *Do you need two negatives here?*

with the other commas in the sentence, wouldn't a stronger mark of punctuation be better?   slapped and scratched. Topsy could turn her hearing off and on to suit her

fancy. If we wanted to comb her, we could yell and scream to no avail͜o but

if she was a mile away͜o and <u>we</u> opened the icebox, she'd be there. Then

she would look at <u>you</u> with those big, sad, brown eyes and <u>you</u> would throw   *who, me?*

her some food. Topsy should have been on the Pirate team. She could

The reader has to puzzle over this sentence to see what it has to do with Topsy.

jump and make a catch in mid-air. (The cat's dish was always empty no

matter how far away we put it.) When (she) was bad she knew it, for she   *Who? the cat?*

would hide under the table. Topsy was a mastermind at opening doors. She

actually figured out that if she turned the knob the door would open. She

would fight any dog, no matter what the size. She was a good mother for a

couple of weeks and then you couldn't get her to go near the pups. Three

dogs and two cats are too many animals, and we were forced to give her

away. And so ends my story of Topsy our first and best dog.

To the Student

Well done! You have written a good paragraph with lots of detail. The reader really gets a picture of Topsy. I have made some suggestions that will help you to improve some of the things that might confuse or bother a reader.

To the Teacher

This student can communicate. With some help she could become a good writer.

Much of what needs to be done to improve this paper would have to be explained in conference. For example, the first and last sentences are literary clichés. This student needs to be encouraged to do throughout what she has done in the body of her theme: express herself in her own language. She should also be shown that she is relying too heavily on compound sentences.

Levels of usage should also be discussed with her. In the fourth sentence, for example, she juxtaposes the informal "yell and scream" with the formal "to no avail." In that same sentence she uses (quite appropriately) the pronoun "we." In the very next sentence, however, she switches to the informal "you."

Finally, the teacher could help this student to see that, if she had thought her material through a little more carefully, she might have organized it into two paragraphs instead of presenting it in one. The second half of her paragraph (beginning with "The cat's dish . . .") might better have been gathered together under a topic sentence about the ways in which Topsy got into trouble or did things that she was not supposed to do.

Grade 8   Good

I'd Like to Win a Contest

Effective choice of specific details

For years I've been coloring pictures, writing jingles, planning dream *Good opening sentence* trips, matching photos of twins, spending imaginary prize money and naming puppies and ponies--but I've never won a contest! My family has cut up Campfire Marshmallows, eaten boxes of cereal, scrubbed with Camay soap, *Effective verbs + nice use of alliteration.* sipped Nescafe, sifted large quantities of Pillsbury flour and slathered Planter's Peanut Butter on countless crackers just to get a label or boxtop, but from all my entries nothing has come.

Good transition Notices about contests seem to come upon me very suddenly and in the most unexpected places. Only last Sunday morning I was quietly reading the *Good choice of adjectives* funnies when I fell prey to glaring, orange headlines announcing: "Teen-agers, *Good development* win your very own telephone!" This contest only required a last line to rhyme with "great" and the end flap from a package of Velveeta. The prize was a telephone in any color of the winner's choice with a private number. Fortunately, there was Velveeta in the refrigerator, so I set to work. I rhymed lines all that day, oblivious to everything around me. I didn't hear the phone ring or the door slam as my brother went out, and when a whole horde of *What does only modify?* relatives arrived from out of town, I (only) poked my head out of my room long enough to say hello, and then went back to pondering again. The only good *You have used three s clauses.* line I could think of ended in the same word as the sample given in the paper, so I discarded that and started all over. Finally I thought I had something *How about some variety?* so I sent it off, full of wild hopes once more. I still haven't heard anything about it, and I'm still tying up the family telephone.

Good transition

    I must be the most unlucky contestant in the country. They never draw my name in the "Lucky Lever Sweepstakes," and I never have the "Lucky Buck." I'm not even lucky in games at home. In Monopoly, when I own the Boardwalk with three hotels, nobody lands there, but when I'm in a tight spot, the Chance card I pick says "Go to jail!" We have a family game of guessing cars. Whenever we're anxious for company to arrive, my brother and I count cars going up and down the street. If I say they will arrive in the tenth

What people? Your guests?

car, the people drive up in the next one that turns the corner. We bet on the colors of cars, too, and when I favor blue ones, only red trucks come past the house. Once I almost won when I said our guests would arrive in the fifth green car, but I didn't know about their new red convertible!

    Even after all these discouragements I continue! Every time I see a contest ad, my old passion comes back and I'm off on another binge. It seems to me that since someone out of all the contestants in the United States, Canada and sometimes the possesions, has to win, it could be me one time! I wonder what color I'd choose for that telephone if.......................!

Effective ending

To the Student

    In this piece of writing you show originality, imagination, and a lively sense of humor. Your use of specific details and illustrations to support your topic sentence is very effective. Your firm, clear transition from one paragraph to another shows careful advance planning of the paper. The ending is cleverly done and in keeping with the tone of the rest of the composition. Try entering a writing contest — sometime!

To the Teacher

    This is excellent work for an eighth grader. The writing has definite style in its maintenance of a light, amusing tone. The topic sentence is well-written with its use of definite examples of contest attempts and the strong contrasting statement of the central idea. The writer chooses details which are specific and appropriate. Her choice of words is good. The transition from one paragraph to the next is smoothly managed. The ending is particularly apt.

This writer demonstrates an excellent mastery of mechanics throughout. Surely no one could object to the colloquial use of "it could be me." There is an error in the placement of the modifier *only*. The repetitive use of the *so* clause mentioned in the interlinear comment can be easily corrected.

Since this writer has a definite flair for this type of writing, she should be encouraged to read widely in the field of informal essays, including such magazines as *Harper's, Atlantic Monthly,* and *The New Yorker.*

Here, evaluators point up the need for logical outlining and limiting topics.

EVALUATING NINTH GRADE STUDENT THEMES°

Illinois English Bulletin

NERO

No doubt you have seen the picture *Quo Vadis,* a picture which is based highly upon the life of Nero, Rome's ruler. I am going to give you my version of Nero. Nero to my belief was insane. He killed his wife and mother after he became ruler of Rome. He said that he knew that the people were calling him a tyrant but he had to kill his wife and mother to prove his power.

He then decided that he would build a new Rome, which would be the center of the universe and he would rule the world from Rome. He sent his soldiers to burn the poorer sections of Rome. While Rome burned the people tried to get away from the flames. Nero stood atop of the courtyard and fiddled. He wanted fire to be more exciting than the one at Troy. The people were rescued from the flames and they rebelled against thier ruler. Nero's wife, was in love with a soldier but the soldier with in love with a Christian girl, this made the ruuler's wife angry, she advised Nero to blame the fire on the Christians. Nero gladly took the advise. The people of Rome then turned against the Christians. Nero sent his soldiers to the Christians grounds to bring the people to the dungeons to await sentence. Thousands of Christians were devoured by lions in the arena. It then came to the people's knowledge that it was Nero who really burned Rome. The people rebelled for the second time. This caused Nero to get panicky. He ran into the palace and asked his servant what to do. She told him he would be better off if he killed himself. Nero was going to stab himself but he didn't have the nerve, the servant had to push the knife in. I suppose you see why I say Nero was insane.

EVALUATION

Quality of content	Fair	Diction	Fair
Originality of treatment	Poor	Grammatical usage	Fair
Unity	Fair	Sentence structure	Poor
Coherence	Fair	Spelling	Fair
Emphasis	Fair	Punctuation	Poor
Paragraphing	Poor		

Median grade: C (3 B, 11 C, 5 D)

COMMENTS TO THE STUDENT

You give more a summary of Nero in simple story action rather than prove he is insane. When you take a theme or idea to defend, you must make the whole writing support that idea — you need not retell the story. You need not even keep the material in time sequence; rather, arrange your evidence or proof to best support your idea.

°From *Illinois English Bulletin,* 40, 6 (March 1953; reprinted November 1962), 16-19, 21-22. Used by permission of *Illinois English Bulletin,* Wilmer A. Lamar, Editor.

You have given an orderly account of Nero's activities, even though you may not have proved his insanity. You could inject more life into your writing by the use of varied sentence beginnings — participial phrases, infinitive phrases, prepositional phrases, and adverbial clauses — instead of always starting with the subject.

Your composition is good except for poor sentence structure. We'll discuss the run-on sentences in class, so that you and others can avoid them in your next writing.

Your sentences are short, choppy, monotonous. The use of complex sentences would make this smoother and more interesting.

Do you remember what we learned about *there* and *their?* We must also watch such tricky nouns and verbs as *advice* and *advise*.

COMMENTS TO TEACHERS

The sentence structure, in many places, is extremely poor. Many sentences like those in this theme may profitably be discussed in class, with the students offering suggestions for improvement.

A simple outline to build on would have been helpful: I believe Nero was insane because — 1. 2. 3.

AVIATION

The curiosity of mankind first started the eagerness to fly. Long ago people thought about flying. They designed ships to fly but never tried them.

The Wright brothers made the first successful flying machine. They first made gliders and tried with much success. Their first flying machine was flown at Kitty Hawk, North Carolina in 1901. A great deal of credit goes to the Wright brothers for the gifts toward Aviation.

Lindberg also made history with the airplane. He was the first one to fly the Atlantic Ocean from New York to France. His plane (Thi Spirit of St. Louis) is now in the museum. Lindberg also recieves a great deal of credit toward aviation.

Airplanes since then have been used for about everything such as war, public service, exploring, and intertainment.

Airplanes have been used mostly for War. In World War I the United States was caught off guard with no planes. They had to buy them from Britain and France. In the beginning of World War 2 the United States had faster, more dependable planes. They were capable of doing 300 m.p.h. armed with heavy machine guns. They had two types of airplanes then: The bomber and the fighter plane. The type bomber they used at the first of the war was the B-19. The B-19 did not have enough range so the A.F. developed the B-29. Its bombay was planty big enough to carry an Atom Bomb which it did. Even the B-29 was not beg enough to reach far away targats. Out of that problem they developed the B-36. The B-36 is capable of carrying a 10,000 pound load 5,000 miles away and returning. But it is not big enough. They are now working on the B-47 Stratojet. It has been made but not put in mass production. The A.F. has also developed the B-52 jet bomber which can make a trip around the world without stopping to refuel. Some other fast jet fighters are the F-86 Sabre jet which is now being used in Korea. It is a proven combat fighter. Others are the XF-91, a high speed interceptor and the F-86D.

It is quite different from the F-86 Sabre jet.

Airplanes have been used as a means of transportation. They are used to ship mail and other goods. C-47's are used mostly for this.

The DC-6 and the DC-4 are well known passenger planes because they are safe and easy to fly.

Aviation is still young and has a great future ahead.

EVALUATION

Quality of content	Good	Diction	Fair
Originality of treatment	Fair	Grammatical usage	Fair
Unity	Fair	Sentence structure	Fair
Coherence	Fair	Spelling	Fair
Emphasis	Fair	Punctuation	Fair
Paragraphing	Fair		

Median grade: C (7 B, 10 C, 2 D)

COMMENTS TO THE STUDENT

The topic which you selected is much too big for one composition. Narrow it down to one phase of aviation, possibly a certain type of plane used in World War II. Reorganize paragraphs throughout the theme, as they are either too long or too short. Observe and correct the mechanical errors that I have marked.

You have taken a rather large topic for your theme — the Wrights, Lindberg, or war aviation would have sufficed. You seem well informed and interested — qualities necessary for good writing. Beware of capitalizing common nouns. You have some careless spelling and vague reference of *they* and *which*. Can you think of a more rousing or interesting title?

Try to vary your sentences. Almost all of them start with the subject.

COMMENTS TO TEACHERS

This student needs help in attaining sentence variety and in making his pronouns agree with their antecedents.

This theme is an example of too large a topic for a small paper. A lesson on limiting topics would be very timely.

Discuss the use of research in writing themes.

Suggest that this student make a simple outline before he writes.

WHAT I LIKE ABOUT SPRING

When the Earth turns and old Sol shines just right, we have the season known as spring. The days grow longer and warmer and old Sol lends his sunny smile to make the weather completely delightful.

Old Mother Nature, who seemed to have been hibernating through the winter months, comes forth in all her glory in her new Easter suit. Her spreading green skirt, the grass, polka-dotted with beautiful spring flowers harmonizes well with her blouse of pink and white fruit blossoms.

In the meadow the ewes graze contentedly while their young lambs scamper about gleefully. There are new piggies, chickens, and even wobbly little calves. The birds, in their flashing new suits, sit in the green leafing trees and give many concerts for one and all.

Even the garden shows life as the seeds take root and tiny plants shoot above the ground.

Yes, everyone one wanders there is that delicious smell and feeling that is enthusiastically received much as a spicy kitchen is on a cool autumn day. Spring is here at last!

EVALUATION

Quality of content	Good	Diction	Good
Originality of treatment	Good	Grammatical usage	Good
Unity	Good	Sentence structure	Good
Coherence	Good	Spelling	Good
Emphasis	Fair	Punctuation	Fair
Paragraphing	Fair		

Median grade: B (3 A, 9 B, 6 C, 1 D)

COMMENTS TO THE STUDENT

After reading your description, I can see Mother Nature in her Easter suit, I can see the meadow, and I can begin to see the garden. However, I am still in doubt as to what you like about spring.

Most words are well chosen; however, "Old Sol" and some other expressions are worn out, and "piggies" sound babyish. Paragraph 4, which is too short, needs expansion.

Interesting experiment with comparisons. Beware of allowing comparisons to become too extravagant, however — there is a fine line between *enough* and *too much.* Your last paragraph is weak; I question the worth of bringing in the reference to autumn.

Your beginning sentence and final paragraph are not clear.

COMMENTS TO TEACHERS

This theme would be a good one to read aloud. Ask the pupils what they think the author meant to say in the beginning and end.

Students who write like this have acquired a large stock of trite or stereotyped words which they pull out without thinking. There should be class discussion of such words and of the value of observation. There is no evidence that this student has ever actually *observed* a spring day; he is merely using expressions that thousands of people have used before.

Use models to teach more effective sentence structure and paragraph development.

Careful revision, coupled with encouragement to the student, will go a long way. So that the teacher and pupil can talk over the pupil's writing, I suggest fewer themes (perhaps one a week) and an insistence on higher quality.

*The authors' consensus in this article is that more attention
must be given to perfecting the paragraph and understanding
of usage through reading and writing assignments. They admit,
too, that the problem of "what grammar to teach" is still in
the stages of transition and urge that teachers keep abreast
of new developments in this area. Finally, they append their
joint findings of the best criteria for evaluating themes and
offer a few samples of student writing against which to measure
them.*

A REPORT: WHAT IS COMPOSITION AT THE NINTH GRADE LEVEL?*

RUSSELL ARTHUR, North Lafayette Junior High School
JOHN GRETENCORD, Tecumseh Junior High, Lafayette
SANDRA JOHNSON, West Lafayette High
ROBERT HUNTING, Purdue (Chairman)

To answer our title question, we first assembled a fairly representative selection of books and articles that dealt either in whole or in part with our problem. We reduced our list to these sources:

BOOKS

The English Language Arts in the Secondary School
(Prepared by the Commission on the English Curriculum of the National Council of Teachers of English)
New York: Appleton-Century-Crofts, Inc., 1956.

Loban, Walter; Margaret Ryan; and James R. Squire
Teaching Language and Literature
New York: Harcourt, Brace and World, Inc., 1961.

Pooley, Robert C., *Teaching English Usage*
New York: Appleton-Century-Crofts, Inc., 1946.

Wolfe, Don M., *Creative Ways to Teach English*, Grades 7-12
New York: The Odyssey Press, 1958.

Sauer, Edwin H., *English in the Secondary School*
New York: Holt, Rinehart and Winston, 1961.

PUBLISHED SYLLABUSES

A Curriculum for English
The Nebraska Council of Teachers of English
Lincoln, Nebraska, 1961.

Communication Series, English, Grades 9-10
Iowa Secondary School Cooperative Curriculum
Issued by the Department of Public Instruction
Published by the State of Iowa, 1948.

---

*From *Standards for Written English in Grade 9, Indiana English Leaflet* 4 (June 1962), 4-12, 20-22, 32-34. Used by permission of Robert Hunting, Chairman.

Digest of Courses of Study for Secondary Schools of Indiana
Department of Public Instruction, Bulletin No. 217, 1954.
Syllabus in English for Secondary Schools, Grades 7 through 12
New York State Education Department, Albany, New York, 1961.

ARTICLES OR PAMPHLETS

Grose, Lois, "Teaching Writing in the Junior High School"
English Journal (February 1960).

Hach, Clarence W., "Needed: A Sequential Program in Composition"
English Journal (November 1960).

"Standards of Achievement in English for Grades 1 through 12"
Kentucky English Bulletin, Vol. 9, No. 1 (Fall 1959).

Strom, Ingrid M., "Research in Grammar and Usage and Its Implications
for Teaching Writing," *Bulletin of the School of Education*,
Indiana University, Vol. 36, No. 5 (September 1960).

From the texts listed above we tried to find answers to two questions: What do authorities recommend that we emphasize in the teaching of 9th grade English? How about grammar and usage in the teaching of composition at this level?

What to Emphasize

All our authorities agree: the main job is to teach the paragraph. Clarence Hach, for example, says, "Begin with a review of the topic outline and a variety of paragraphs, chiefly expository and descriptive."[1] Mr. Hach believes that 9th graders should then progress to the two-paragraph themes — thus students would get experience with the problem of transitions — and finally to the "short five-paragraph themes."[2]

Syllabuses of Iowa[3] and New York[4] also put emphasis on training the student to write paragraphs. So too does the Indiana *Digest of Courses of Study:* the objective in the teaching of "written expression" is in this document defined as being "to form clear, concise, correct sentences and to develop them into simple, unified paragraphs."[5]

Edwin Sauer contributes substantially the same thought: 9th grade students should "have a sense of the paragraph as the *rounded development* [his italics] of an idea."[6] The *Kentucky English Bulletin* projects much the same kind of program.[7]

Professor Sauer — and also the Iowa syllabus — recommend that some student writing be impromptu. Iowa likes the idea of "Two or three impromptu papers

---

[1]"Needed: A Sequential Program in Composition," *English Journal* (November 1960), 540.
[2]P. 43.
[3]*Communication Series, English, Grades* 9-10, Issued by the Department of Public Instruction and published by the State of Iowa, 1958, p. 67.
[4]*Syllabus in English for Secondary Schools, Grades 7 through* 12, New York State Education Department, Albany, New York, 1961, pp. 127-128.
[5]Department of Public Instruction, Bulletin No. 217, 1954, p. 43.
[6]*English in the Secondary School*, New York, 1961, p. 110.
[7]"Standards of Achievement in English for Grades 1 through 12," Vol. 9, No. 1 (Fall 1959), p. 29.

as tests of the development of habitual skills";[8] Sauer says, "That a large part of the composition work should be impromptu is also generally accepted now — personally, I think one-fourth a desirable amount."[9]

The consensus seems clear. Teachers in 9th grade English classes should emphasize the writing of the paragraph. Moreover, to do any good, the writing must be frequent. Lois Grose asks, "How often is 'frequent'?" and answers "Nobody can alter the basic truth that the only way to learn to write is to write, and write often."[10] Nebraska's *A Curriculum For English* remarks that "If the junior high student is to achieve any competence in composition . . . , then surely the teacher must assign each semester at least twelve short papers."[11] Our Indiana Standards Committee agrees with this conclusion. In fact, we urge that some writing be done every week. Furthermore, we like to think that training in the writing of the *expository* paragraph is generally a very good thing — though at the same time we are pleased to find none of our experts arguing that 9th grade writing should be limited only to exposition.

Other interesting points emerge from this study. For example, Mr. Hach thinks that the 9th grade is a good time to introduce students to the type of paragraph needed to answer a simple essay question.[12] Also, the so-called "practical" assignments continue to be advised: *e.g.*, the informal courtesy note and the personal letter;[13] précis writing;[14] and the "autobiography."

Of course many of the skills mentioned above are taught concurrently with a unit or as part of a unit.[16]

How about Grammar and Usage?

The most specific aid we found is that given by Robert Pooley in *Teaching English Usage*. This book has a very helpful list of "Errors to be attacked for Elimination in the Junior High School," and "Forms to Receive No Class Instruction in the Junior High School."[17]

Speaking more generally, we learned that opinion seems to be moving clearly toward one conclusion in what was once a very explosive area: i.e., we learned that the most effective teaching of grammar and usage is that which is done in

---

[8]P. 67.

[9]P. 88.

[10]"Teaching Writing in the Junior High School," *English Journal* (February 1960), P. 90.

[11]The Nebraska Council of Teachers of English, Lincoln, Nebraska, 1961, p. 39C.

[12]P. 541.

[13]*Communication Series* (Iowa), pp. 78-90. Note: We reject the idea of the personal letter because, *as a class assignment*, it presents the student with an artificial and obviously unrealistic writing problem.

[14]*Syllabus in English* (New York) p. 128; *Digest of Courses of Study* (Indiana), p. 43.

[15]*See, e.g.*, Wolfe, Ch. 7. Note: We believe the term *autobiography* as used by Wolfe and others is misleading. The writing-problems posed by an autobiography have been mastered by only a few men: one thinks of Cellini, Rousseau, Franklin, Trollope. A 9th grader can do no more than fumble with so gigantic a problem. We suggest calling the 9th grader's "autobiography" what it really is: a "personal experience theme" or a "familiar essay."

[16]*See e.g., passim* in Wolfe; Loban, Ryan, and Squire; the *Communication Series* (Iowa); *A Curriculum for English* (Nebraska).

[17]*Teaching English Usage*, New York, 1946, pp. 194-98: 218-23.

conjunction with reading and writing assignments. Thus Grose: "This [junior high] is the time to teach mechanics. The same pupils who have developed . . . the ability to 'tune out' boring drill and discussion of principles of grammar . . . will come to life mentally and learn rules . . . as they are needed to express the important things they have to say."[18] Thus, also, the Iowa syllabus: "[The teacher] is advised to teach grammar . . . by connecting it with the needs of the class as revealed by the corrections on their papers."[19] Thus, too, Loban, Ryan, and Squire: "No matter how good a teacher's intentions, the classifications [composition, spelling, oral communication, etc.] tend to be self-contained, diminishing valuable relationships and support from other aspects of English. Furthermore, the classifications, although unquestionably determined by the nature of the discipline, lack vitality for most of the learners. . . ."[20]

Finally, on the question, "WHAT grammar to teach?" our committee believes that it must adopt a wait-and-see attitude. At least it is in part a wait-and-see attitude. To be sure, the evidence of numerous studies has conclusively resolved one problem. That is, as Ingrid Strom reports: "The research findings show clearly and overwhelmingly that direct methods of instruction, focusing on writing activities and the structuring of ideas, are more efficient in teaching sentence structure, usage, punctuation, and other related factors than are such methods as nomenclature drill, diagraming, and rote memorization of grammatical rules."[21] However, if we are not to teach "nomenclature drill, diagraming, and rote memorization of grammatical rules," what kind of grammar, if any, should we teach? The committee does not believe that our profession has many answers that are, as yet, satisfactory to any but minority groups. Dedicated and serious and knowledgeable people are at work on this problem. The confusion will no doubt resolve itself, in time. In the interim, while we "wait and see," we have these recommendations: (1) Admit frankly that we are in an awkward period of transition and ask our friends (principals, superintendents, editors, members of the PTA, etc.) to be patient with us while we work this thing out; (2) Keep ourselves informed of developments in this subject (reading the best journals and books; attending workshops and conferences, etc.); (3) Continue to help students to earn competence in such essential matters as standards of generally accepted good usage and a command of the basic sentence patterns of their language; (4) As we try to teach young people to write, we ought to remember this tested conclusion: "Children and adolescents improve their sentences by having many opportunities, with the guidance of the teacher, for structuring their own thoughts into their own sentences."[22]

---

[18]"Teaching Writing in the Junior High School," p. 67.
[19]*Communication Series*, p. 67.
[20]*Teaching Language and Literature*, p. 10.
[21]Ingrid M. Strom, "Research in Grammar and Usage and Its Implications for Teaching Writing," *Bulletin of the School of Education*, Indiana University, Vol. 36, No. 5 (September 1960), pp. 13-14.
[22]*Ibid*, p. 14.

Criteria* to Be Used in Grading Themes

INTENTION

intelligently limited in subject matter

clearly apparent to the writer

interesting to the writer

worth the writer's effort to communicate; and worth the reader's effort to understand

relevant to the assignment given

ORGANIZATION

theme is clearly planned; the writing is so organized as to support the writer's purpose

DEVELOPMENT

sufficient supporting material

(That is, the intention of the paragraph or theme is adequately supported by example, incident, reasons, comparison and/or contrast, etc.)

supporting material obviously relevant to the purpose of the paragraph or theme

EXPRESSION

Diction

meaningful (coherent)

appropriate to purpose and situation

idiomatic

Mechanics (Spelling, grammar, punctuation)

contribute to the fulfillment of the writer's purpose and to the reader's enjoyment of the writing

APPEARANCE

neat, legible

required format (with respect to margins, method of folding paper, *etc.*) observed

THEME 1

Assignment: Tell about a "dragon" you would like to slay.

A DRAGON I'D LIKE TO SLAY

	Lines
I cast a furtive glance over my shoulder and stole around the	1
corner of the house. So far, so good. Working quietly, I squeezed	2
lemon juice all over my face and buried the mangled lemon directly	3
behind me. The battle of the freckles was on again!	4
I crept back to bed and fell asleep. The next morning when I	5
awoke, I rushed to the mirror, but nothing had happened. My freckles	6
were still there!	7
From early childhood, I have been plagued with the so-called "marks	8
of beauty." Up to the seventh grade, I didn't mind my freckles; I just	9

---

*These are intended to be thought of as criteria for an "A" paragraph or theme by a student in the academic program.

shrugged them off. But when I entered Tecumseh, something in my — 10
adolescent brain snapped. All at once I couldn't stand the sight of — 11
them. I blushed every time they were mentioned, I cried over them, and — 12
wailed about them to my family. — 13

As I grew older, I began to build up a resistance to the teasing — 14
about them, and stopped thinking so much about them. By my freshman — 15
year, I was resigned to the fact that they were "here to stay." — 16

Now I don't worry about them nearly as much as I did, and when — 17
someone teases me, I just laugh it off. I've almost given up the idea — 18
of losing them, but maybe someday. . . . — 19

GRADES				GOOD	FAIR	POOR
A	14*		Intention	23*	1	
B	9		Organization	17*	4	2
C	3		Development	18	3*	3
D	2		Expression			
F	0		Diction	15	6*	
			Mechanics	16*	5	2

*Committee grade

Marginal Comments

COMMENTS WORTH NOTING	COMMENTS THAT WOULD BE OF LITTLE OR NO HELP TO THE STUDENT
Title	Avoid contractions.
	Tie your title in with the theme.
	The title applies only to the first paragraph.
Line	
1	Why go outside?
2 The fragment is effective. You might use an asterisk to indicate that the fragment is deliberately used—for rhetorical effect—and not the result of ignorance.	Fragment Your exaggeration is not convincing.
3	*Mangled* is the wrong word. Change *mangled* to *squashed*.
4 You describe an action which clearly demonstrates that the "battle is on." You do not have to *say* that it is on. Therefore, omit the last sentence of paragraph one, and	*Me* should be omitted.
5 join paragraphs one and two.	

6

Comma sufficient. Omit *but*.
No comma after *mirror*.
Use a period after *mirror* and omit
but.
Use a semicolon after *mirror*.

8 *From* is the wrong word here. Try
since.
Omit comma after *childhood*.

9 A slight contradiction of the pre-
ceding sentence.
Change *up to* to *until*.
Omit the comma after *grade*.

The period should go outside the
quotes.
Unnecessary quotation marks.

10 Can a person *shrug off* freckles?

The sentence beginning with *but* is a
fragment.
Use *however*, instead.
Omit *but*. Begin with *when*.
This seems a little crude.

11

Spell out contractions.
Use a comma after *once*.

12

Omit *I* in second item of the series.
Comma splice
Use semicolons and include *I*.

13 To achieve parallel construction,
insert *I* in third part of series.

Cried and *wailed* are repetitious.

14

Awkward sentence
[EDITORS' COMMENT: You do not help the
student, usually, until you tell him *what*
is awkward.]

15 "About them" is repetitious.

End sentence at *them*.
Begin with *I*.
Place periods outside quotes.

16 Omit comma after year.

17 No need to begin a new paragraph.

We generally use *so* after negative.
[EDITORS' NOTE: Good usage no longer re-
quires *so* after a negative.]
Change the comma to a semicolon.
Omit *and*. Begin with *when*.

18

The paragraph is weakened by the
overuse of weak words like *almost,
maybe, nearly*.
It has no antecedent.

19

The final idea (that you no longer
worry) is a contradiction of the beginning incident,

General Comments at the End of the Theme

COMMENTS WORTH NOTING

Just in time, with your last sentence, you bring us back to the original intention.

The plunge-in beginning is good. Because the topic is rather informal, the informality of the diction is appropriate.

There are colorful spots in the diction (*furtive, plagued, snapped*) but there are some clichés ("something in my brain snapped"; "couldn't stand the sight of").

The fragment is an effective one. The attempt at parallelism and the use of the semicolon indicate a better-than-average understanding of mechanics.

The time of the opening incident is hazy; consequently, we sense a slight contradiction at the end. If the incident at the beginning occurred recently, as it seems to, how is it that you no longer "worry nearly as much as you did"?

The changing point of view is an interesting method of unfolding your theme.

You have a tendency to overpunctuate; the commas are not really necessary after an introductory prepositional phrase.

COMMENTS THAT WOULD BE OF LITTLE OR NO HELP TO THE STUDENT

The theme lacks unity.

The metaphor is not sustained. The theme lacks coherence.

Your story lacks distinctive style i.e. otained [sic] by a large vocabulary and different kinds of sentences as to meaning.

There is no logical relationship of ideas. The material is not ordered effectively.

The dragon is your freckles, I take it. The title is applicable to paragraph one only.

Last two paragraphs show an exaggeration or a cynical point of view.

Avoid contractions.

You are developing the right idea toward your freckles.

This story has a newspaper approach.

THEME 2

Assignment: Develop a paragraph, using, as your first sentence, the following: There are many kinds of faces in the world.

THE MANY FACES OF MAN

	Lines
There are many different kinds of faces in the world. There are	1
faces that express hate or happiness. But most of them are happy	2
faces. Have you every heard of the man on the street? Well, someday	3
just watch someplace where thier are a lot of people like downtown	4
or a shopping or the best place would be a race track. They would	5
be different of course their are faces of men who do hard labor of	6
course their's would be like sandpaper beards and wrinkles and crackes.	7
So sometime just notice the many different kinds of faces on earth.	8

GRADES			GOOD	FAIR	POOR
A	0	Intention	3	16*	9
B	0	Organization		6	23*
C	2	Development		4	25*
D	13	Expression			
F	14*	Diction		4	25*
		Mechanics			29

*Committee grade

Marginal Comments

COMMENTS WORTH NOTING

Line

1 Although you lead us to believe you are going to show us many different kinds of faces, you really show us only one (line 7). Rewrite this theme as your next assignment, describing several types of faces.

[EDITORS' NOTE: We believe this is the most relevant comment to make here.]

2

3

4 You need to study the difference between *their, there — were* and *where.*

Sp.

5

COMMENTS THAT WOULD BE OF LITTLE OR NO HELP TO THE STUDENT

The word *different* does not appear in the assigned sentence.

Insert *some* before *faces,* a comma after *hate,* and *others that express* before *happiness.*

Don't start a sentence with *but.*

awkward
extraneous
Avoid using *well* at the beginning of a sentence.

Change to "people in a downtown area, or a better place might be a race track."
a lot of: colloquial

Restate the sentence.

6 Sentences run together. Sp.	K
7 Sp. Possessive pronouns do not use an apostrophe.	Change *be like* to *show*.
8	Don't start a sentence with *so*. Change *on earth* to *people around you*.

General Comments at the End of the Theme

COMMENTS WORTH NOTING

The writer has no exact idea of what he wants to say. There is no evidence of real thought and sincerity. He should first choose a place where he will see a variety of faces—in the study hall, for instance. He should look at them carefully to see how they differ as to general expression and as to detail. He should report his conclusions honestly, organized in some sensible manner (by types).

Try reading this aloud. What about the *man on the street?* What about the differences? What do they tell you? You describe only one kind of face.

Lines 6 and 7 introduce an interesting picture. I wish you had spent more time developing this idea.

COMMENTS THAT WOULD BE OF LITTLE OR NO HELP TO THE STUDENT

Can you meet with me during sixth period? I'd like to go over this with you. I have not indicated all the errors.

[EDITORS' NOTE: The teacher put about 25 pejorative comments of one sort or another on this student's paper. Now she wants to meet the student so that, apparently, she can point out other errors which she had not indicated. We would not blame the student for not looking forward to the conference.]

You didn't even follow directions.

You definitely did not proofread.

The question in line 3 seems to have little connection with the rest.

This student does not have sufficient command of mechanics to write a paragraph. He should concentrate on basic sentence structure.

Too many errors exist for a teacher to spend time to grade them. This student needs more help than the average classroom teacher can give him. Seemingly no organization or development. Lacks conclusion.

Study carefully the rules governing the use of the comma.

THEME 3

SCHOOLS OFFER MORE THAN AN EDUCATION

	Lines
"History is so boring. I think I'll study art." This person is	1
unfortunately, a victim of misplaced emphasis in our schools. Art is im-	2
portant; but is it more important than history? Definitely not! Yet	3
how is this person to know? No one is there to recommend history, and	4
probably no one would tell him in school. He is lost in a sea of knowledge.	5
School offers far too many subjects, and the importance of the more essen-	6
tial ones is soon no longer stressed. The pupil makes his own choice as	7
to which courses he will study and, in many cases, picks the easier, less	8
challenging ones. He is thus limiting his own education. This, of course,	9
would not occur if so many subjects were not available in the first place.	10
Schools, unfortunately, offer more than a good education.	11

GRADES			GOOD	FAIR	POOR
A	3*	Intention	12*	15	3
B	11	Organization	8*	13	9
C	11	Development	5	15*	10
D	4	Expression			
F	0	Diction	13*	15	1
		Mechanics	19*	11	

*Committee grade: A—

Marginal Comments

COMMENTS WORTH NOTING

Title

Line	
1 What person? Substitute "The person who says this is . . ."	
2	
3	
[EDITORS' NOTE: A teacher may request students to indicate fragments, with asterisks. That is, she may quite validly insist that there is a difference between a deliberate fragment and an accidental one, composed in ignorance.]	
4 *What* person?	

COMMENTS THAT WOULD BE OF LITTLE OR NO HELP TO THE STUDENT

The writer has interpreted *more than* as being too much of the same, rather than *other than*.

Write out contractions.
Put *unfortunately* at the beginning of the sentence.

Does any school emphasize art over history?

Change semicolon to comma.
Change semicolon to period; capitalize *but*.
Fragment
SS
[EDITORS' NOTE: We think this symbol—like K—gives little help to the student.]

there: where?
No one is vague. Use *teacher,* or some other definite noun.
how . . . know extraneous.
[EDITORS' QUERY: Why *extraneous*?]

5 incomplete: *tell him* what? *Sea of knowledge* is misleading and interrupts the train of thought. *Sea of knowledge* is trite.

Lines four and five criticize the school and do not develop the topic. See the title.
misplaced phrase (*in school*)
Transition is needed.
Clarify *no one . . . knowledge.*
[EDITORS' QUERY: The sentence seems clear enough to us.]
knowledge—WW

6 Change *school offers* to *schools offer* for consistency. (See title & line 11)
Name a few subjects.

Restate this sentence.
Transition
More?

7 Omit *soon.*

K
I know of no school where a pupil has complete freedom to choose the courses which will lead to his graduation from high school.
awkward transition

8

How many cases?
Put comma before *and,* not after.
Omit commas before and after *in many cases.*
Omit comma after *and.*

9 A careful writer would pinpoint *this* and not refer vaguely to the entire thought preceding it.

From line 8 through line 10, you leave the topic.
Better as one sentence.
Put *thus* before *he* and set off with commas, omitting period after *ones.*
Sub.
The reasoning of line 10 is questionable.

10

available in the first place is never shown.

11

weak clincher.
a guidance solution would be stronger.
In line 11, do you mean *unfortunately?*
Not quite true.
extraneous conclusion

General Comments at the End of the Theme

COMMENTS WORTH NOTING

You lack specific, concrete material. You need greater development of your subject.

The paragraph presents a provocative angle to the subject. However, insufficient evidence of proof leaves the reader in a controversial state of mind. Let's have a debate!

You have over-simplified the problem you wrote about.

You made many generalizations. Unless you show the reader (by facts, statistics, or references to other authorities) that you know whereof you write, do not assume you are qualified to state your opinion and assumptions as *truths*.

You have excellent control of your sentences; your intention is very clear.

Your metaphor in line 5 is misleading. How is the metaphor pertinent?

COMMENTS THAT WOULD BE OF LITTLE OR NO HELP TO THE STUDENT

[You] refute the proposed topic in *of misplaced emphasis* in line 2 and in *art is more important than history* in line 3.

Negative point of view is expressed from the beginning.

Student does not develop the proposed topic.

Too many extraneous ideas.

Transitions are abrupt; no straightline development exists.

Your theme shows need for organization and thought.

Method of development is rather awkward.

Your opening sentence is ill-chosen and your final sentence doesn't fit at all.

A fragment should fail a composition automatically.

This pupil's information seems a little sketchy.

Lines 6-10 might have been strong at the beginning.

I assume line 11 is your topic sentence. If so, you seem to lack emphasis in building to it.

Do we not have student counselors who help the student plan his schedule wisely?

Have you solved the problem in the best way?

The reader assumes the intention is clear to the writer only through inference.

The support becomes obvious only by guessing at the intention.

I cannot connect the title with the content

The value of the first papers in this group of themes lies in the conciseness of the assignments and the clear-cut reasons outlined by the college evaluators for each theme's success or failure. Not all the papers are top-grade material — an added value aspect since teachers want to know what the colleges call C work, as well as A or B. Abstract topics, as well as assignments drawn from literary subjects, add to the variety here.

RATING AND ANALYSIS OF STUDENT THEMES°

ARNO L. BADER

WILLIAM R. STEINHOFF

Grade: A

Assignment: Choose any three of these four: politics, education, art, religion; demonstrate the continuity, the basic harmoniousness, of your views on each of the three.

THREE POWERS AND THEIR GOALS

Art, education and religion are to me the three civilizing factors in man's existence. Together they have raised him from his primitive state, and together, if we permit them to function fully, they can achieve for man an even finer life. I feel, however, that these three great influences on our growth are not always used to our greatest advantage, because they many times are *not* permitted to function completely.

I believe the Arts can accomplish two things, they can entertain us by furnishing us with experiences we usually don't find in our daily practical lives; and they can broaden us by sharpening our ability to feel and think. It seems to me, however, that the Arts cannot accomplish this second, much greater end unless, in every painting we look at and every book we read, we are given something to feel and think about. I feel, then, that art, to function successfully, should represent a level higher than our own, and that we should work toward that level. When we ask the Arts, as we often do, to descend to our particular understanding, we are reducing them to mere entertainment and cheating ourselves of their greater value.

In the Detroit Institute of Arts is a mural by Diego Rivera which I can neither understand nor, at present, like. The figures are grotesque; they call up several unpleasant ideas in my mind and give me feelings which I can't explain. I've looked at the mural many times and will probably puzzle over it many times more. I may never grow to like it and may never be able to understand it, yet I will always appreciate it. Instead of merely entertaining me, as it might have done, the mural has made me feel and is still making me think. This, I feel, is what all art must do to continue its contribution to the growth of man.

°From Arno L. Bader and William R. Steinhoff, *Preparation for College English, Parts I and II* (Ann Arbor: University of Michigan Press, 1958), pp. 36-47. Used by permission of Arno L. Bader.

Education, to endure as a humanizing element in man's existence, should, I believe, "develop in each individual the knowledge, interest, ideals, habits and powers whereby he will find his place and use that place to shape both himself and his society toward ever nobler ends."[1] Our schools seem to be responding too exclusively to the age's need for specialization, and education, I feel, is becoming primarily a means to support ourselves. Doctors, engineers and chemists are often beginning their careers with insufficient knowledge of those things that contribute greatly toward making the "nobler ends" possible — the arts. Even those in Liberal Arts fields are limited. The art program in this university is so organized that, in my four years here, I will have but three English courses, only one of which will be literature. I will leave also still knowing nothing about music.

As a possible remedy, I would like to see our schools experiment with a required Humanities course to begin in the elementary grades and continue through college. Perhaps this extended study might provide the student with sufficient knowledge of music, literature and the other arts to enable him to actively participate in them throughout his adult life. Education should not only equip us with the means for a successful practical life. It should also, I feel, provide us to the same extent with the means for an intellectual, aesthetic and spiritual life.

In his essay *Religion and Science*, Alfred North Whitehead states, "Religion is tending to degenerate into a decent formula wherewith to embellish a comfortable life". Religion today does seem to me to be straying farther and farther away from its original goal: the union of man's soul with his God in the afterworld. From what I have seen, religion is becoming, instead, primarily concerned with today's world. People seem to be praying less and less for union with God in the hereafter and more and more for things, for health or for success. When people pray today for Heaven, many times it is more from the fear of Hell rather than for Heaven itself. Today religion seems to me to be valued most highly as a way to mental comfort in troubled times and as a way to free ourselves of our feelings of guilt. Even clergymen are stressing the peace of mind aspect of religion. I, too, believe that religion should provide us with a moral code and with spiritual comfort, but above all, I would have religion provide us with its greater value of uniting us with God.

COMMENT (TO THE STUDENT)

This is a superior essay. It sets forth ideas of some complexity and worth on a serious subject — and it is well organized. The word "civilizing" in the opening sentence strikes the keynote. The phrase "elevate man to his highest state" in the closing sentence shows how the concept "civilizing" has been enriched by the intervening paragraphs. Your description of the effect of Rivera's murals makes vivid your conception of the function of art. You have effectively linked art and education by emphasizing the Humanities. Nevertheless, the two paragraphs on Education are somehow not as clear and emphatic as those on Art. You neatly avoided the "embellishment" view of religion. Is the reference to the "afterworld" necessary to your conception of religion as set forth in the paragraph, for you do seem to mean "uniting with God" here and now (as well as in the afterworld) to be the true "elevating of man to his highest state."

---

[1]*Cardinal Principles of Secondary Education*, P. 9 U.S. Bureau of Education, Bulletin 35, 1918.

Grade: D

Assignment: Define an abstract term and use it in an argumentative paper.

Tolerance

The word tolerance when used by people today is usually associated with racial or religious differences. Intolerance pertains to anyone who discriminates unfairly against a persons opinions or beliefs. Therefore if a person is to be tolerant he must be open minded by considering opinions opposite of his. This does not mean that he has to agree with that opinion, but he should show respect for that opinion.

A tolerant person can not be a person who is prejudiced. That is one of the reasons why people always associate tolerance with religious and racial prejudice. Another reason why people associate these two problems with tolerance is the important part they have played in our world and national affairs in the last few years. World War II was nothing more than a war against races and religions. Adolf Hitler believed that the world should be ruled by Aryans. He presecuted the Jews because he wanted to rid the world of nonaryans, and in his mind the Jews were nonaryans. Hitler was certainly not a tolerant person or he would not have looked upon any group as being superior to another. A tolerant person might have not agreed with their ideas or opinions, but he certainly would not persecute them for that reason. In the United States we also have racial problems. The Ku Klux Klan is very intolerant in the way it advocates the discrimination of races and religions. In the south the Klan persecutes the Negroes for being black. When a Negro committs a crime he is seldome tried by a jury of his own perrs since few Negroes are on juries in the southern states. Some Negroes are not even given a trial because enraged whites take the law in their own hands and a lynching is the result. A tolerant person would not take these drastic actions even though he knew the person was guilty of the crime.

The problem of religious toleration is not as prominent as it was during the middle ages, but it is still a very controversial issue. In Spain when they had the inquisition people were persecuted for their religious beliefs. In France the Huguenots were persecuted by the Catholics and were forced to leave France. In the United States we have religious problems which have been held over from the middle ages, for many people discriminate against the Catholics and Jews. Hitler was prejudice against these religions also. Therefore World War II was also a religious conflict. There is a difference of opinion as to whether the Jewish people are considered a race or a religion, and this difference has not been decided because there are many people which believe in both as was proved in World War II. If there had been tolerance among the nations this war might not have been fought.

But there is also other types of tolerance. There is tolerance of ignorance. Even though a person is not as well educated as another he should not be looked down upon as an inferior person. Tolerance of social standing is another one of the worlds problems. In the United States many people are snubbed because they are not in high society. In Europe tolerance of social standing is more of a problem than it is here because they have more distinct class systems, although these class systems are decreasing rapidly. In both these types of tolerance one group looks down upon the other group as being inferior, and in this way they are intolerant.

Thus a tolerant person should be one who is without prejudice or discrimination. A tolerant person should be open-minded and not think anyone as inferior to him because of race, creed, or position. I believe that we must have tolerance if we are to have a happy and peaceful world. Tolerance means understanding and if we had better understanding among nations and peoples a lot of our trouble and problems would be solved.

COMMENT (TO THE STUDENT)

The opinions you express here will be shared by many readers, and they may admire your sympathy for the victims of intolerance. These attitudes come through fairly well. Still, your theme suffers from faults which deprive it of force and persuasiveness. How is your essay constructed? You begin with a definition of tolerance, and then drift into an historical discussion which you follow by general statements about "other types of tolerance." Where do you specify the essential element in tolerance? If a "decent respect" for the opinions of others is your criterion, you should connect this specifically with the conduct you approve or disapprove. The many mechanical errors here (in spelling, reference of pronouns, agreement of subject and verb) distract the reader's attention from what you are saying, and in some readers this may lead to doubt about the quality of what you are saying. Bring your Handbook to the next conference, and we will do some of the exercises together.

Grade: A

Assignment: Write a description of some community that you know well. Try to get below the surface and give some account of the quality of the inner life of the community.

BATCHAWANA VILLAGE

Anyone viewing Batchawana Village, an Indian community in northern Ontario, from a boat or an airplane would be intrigued by its picturesque, rather romantic appearance. Located on one of the vast bays of Lake Superior, it is surrounded by the rocky foothills of the Laurentian Plateau. Its houses perch comfortably on the rugged shoreline, clustering around a tiny church which stands stark white against the dark green trees. Here is a scene one might find on one of those postal cards circulated all over Canada and stamped in the lower left hand corner with the name of a gas station, hotel, restaurant, or tourist resort which invariably is hundreds of miles from the spot pictured.

At close range the village is much less picturesque. The houses string along a dusty gravel road which runs from one end of the eel-like community to the other. Built of tar paper, scrap lumber, and sections from billboards which once urged motorists to "Smoke Sweet Caporals," their unscreened doors and windows yawn open from May until October. Among the weeds under the omnipresent grey laundry in each yard one might find the stripped-down skeleton of an ancient car, a pile of discarded fishing nets heterogeneously tangled with tin cans and empty bottles, a mound of rock specimens, several dirty, nearly naked children, and a motley assortment of mongrel dogs which run howling after each passing vehicle or pedestrian. The two stores in the village offer gasoline, a meager selection of groceries, and whatever clothing the inhabitants have need of. One of the stores is also a post office, defunct save for one day a month when the entire male population descends upon it in a jostling multitude to claim their government checks. Across the road from the post office a barn-like building displays the sign, "Movies Every Friday Night." This motion-picture palace also serves as a school for the few children who do not attend the Catholic school farther down the road and as a church when the Protestant circuit-preacher pays a rare visit to Batchawana. The economic activity of the village centers around a decaying wooden dock where a few leaky fishing boats strain at their ropes. Fishing is the major occupation of that minor faction of the population which cares to work. Occasionally a strange boat docks here: a government cruiser manned by Mounted Police, a wealthy vacationer's yacht, or a lumber steamer. In the last event ten or fifteen recruits spend several days maneuvering a few cords of logs from the shore to the side of the boat with long, spiked poles. Since the lumber production of the village depends upon the individual initiative of the villagers, this occurs only once or twice a year.

These people scarcely remind one of their fiercely proud, fearless ancestors that history books describe as the first inhabitants of our continent. The men crouch contentedly on their plank stoops watching the aimless flight of the gulls. Their families subsist on the monthly charity of the Canadian government, land payments to which they are entitled as descendants of the original owners of that territory. Occasionally they supplement this scanty dole by guiding a hunting or fishing party, cutting pulpwood for a few days, or fighting a nearby forest fire. Fat, toothless women appear only briefly at their doors to squint at the mountains across the bay before they again disappear into the unlit interiors of their squalid houses. Only the ubiquitous children show any signs of exuberance or activity. They splash among the reeds in the shallow water, ride antique bicycles, fish with homemade poles on the dock, and carry on endless cowboy and Indian battles which, incidentally, the Indians invariably win.

Each summer a few tourists come to Batchawana; some to buy supplies and others merely to see an Indian village. The crudely lettered signs advertising fishing guides, fresh lake trout, or angle worms may prompt the travellers to stop, but when their inquiries are met with sullen stares and grunted replies, they speedily abandon the village. The little boys gather around the bright-colored automobiles in admiring groups, their brown eyes shining and small dark fingers caressing the smooth fenders while the small girls whisper excitedly and point at the women's clothing. Some of the teen-agers and young adults are equally affected by this glimpse of the world outside the village. Many of them leave for the city, returning after they encounter the insurmountable wall of prejudice dividing Indians from the rest of the Canadian people. But the older people are impervious to the allure of the cities, scornful of the adventuresome youths, and contented with their uncomplicated existence in Batchawana Village.

Comment

This is a very good paper indeed. It fulfills the assignment admirably, for the writer penetrates into the inner life of the community so that the reader sees the tragedy caused by the clash of two civilizations. The writer shows real skill in presenting authentic and convincing details which make his point for him. The whole paper shows an ease and control which are seemingly the natural outcome of thoughtful observation.

Grade: C+

Assignment: Contrast the treatment of conflict by Willa Cather and Joseph Conrad in "Neighbor Rosicky" and "The Lagoon."

CONFLICTS

Willa Cather and Joseph Conrad realized the importance of conflicts when they wrote "Neighbor Rosicky" and "The Lagoon," for both stories are concerned with an individuals conflicts', his reactions to them, and their effect on his life.

The character, and a study of him, is of primary importance in each tale. The fact that the basic conflict is not present and is related at the time of the story tends to de-emphaize the plot. It is interesting to note that while most of the action centers around Rosicky and Arsat the importance of the other characters differs in each story. Cather takes a lot of time to tell about the many subordinate characters and to contrast them to Rosicky, while in Arsat's story we learn about the other people from him, and the reader is not really given a chance to judge them on the basis of their conversation or present actions. The role of the woman is a good example of differing techniques in story telling. Diamelen is merely a symbol of Arsat's love in "The Lagoon"; however, Mrs. Rosicky is early described as a somewhat rough country girl who is happy helping and being with other people. The few contrasts in the Rosicky's characters and the many similarities are mentioned early in the story. The reasons for the differences which the authors exhibit in the handling of minor characters might be accounted for because Rosicky's conflict of living in the country or city is more of a social problem than Arsat's personal conflict between love and honor. Arsat was primarily interested in how he could best make himself happy when he tried to solve his problem. While Rosicky reached and passed Arsat's goal and turned out to be most interested in doing what he felt would benefit others.

There are not only conflicts between each author's main character and his set of values but also between each author's philosophy of life. Through Rosicky, Willa Cather expresses the belief that problems can be solved by returning to a simpler way of life. Her constant emphasis on the virtues of country life and the fact that Rosicky dies happy point out her sentiments. Her feeling that competitivness is not to be desired are shown by telling how much more happy Rosicky and his family were than other ones who constantly worried about getting ahead.

Conrad, on the other hand, presents a much more complex view of life. By showing that Arsat was not happier following the simpler way of life, the author expresses his own opinions. Arsat learns that although one may achieve happiness for a short time by escaping it, it will not be a lasting happiness. In the end Arsat's realization that he has caused his brother's death, lost honor, and ruined the remainder of his life merely for a few months of pleasure is characteristic of the author's philosophy. In short, Cather feels that happiness can be found by a return to the simpler ways of life, while Conrad does not give a final answer but is against escapism as a way of solving problems.

COMMENT

The principal merit of this paper is that the writer understands what contrast means. He deals first with general aspects of the contrast, then draws conclusions based in part on the evidence he has presented. A second virtue of the paper is that the writer keeps the two stories at the forefront of his own and the reader's attention; justified or not, his opinions are based on the stories to which he constantly refers.

This student, however, has permitted his interest in contrast to lead him away from the specific question of conflict. He is more than halfway through his essay before he defines the conflicts in each story, and he digresses at times to discuss contrasts between characters and techniques without showing how they affect these conflicts. There are here a fragmentary sentence, subjects that do not agree with their verbs, and punctuation errors. These weaknesses are not to be overlooked, of course, but the solidity of the paper gives promise that the writer will not have much difficulty in correcting them.

This paper, written by a high school junior, exemplifies college standards not only in the evaluation but also in the four directives given the student and his manner of handling them.

POETRY ANALYSIS FROM END-OF-YEAR EXAMS*

CEEB Commission on English

I

The broken pillar of the wing jags from the clotted
    shoulder,
The wings trail like a banner in defeat,
No more to use the sky forever but live with famine
And pain a few days: cat nor coyote
Will shorten the week of waiting for death, there
    is game without talons.
He stands under the oak-bush and waits
The lame feet of salvation; at night he remembers
    freedom
And flies in a dream, the dawns ruin it.
He is strong and pain is worse to the strong,
    incapacity is worse.
The curs of the day come and torment him
At distance, no one but death the redeemer will
    humble that head,
The intrepid readiness, the terrible eyes.
The wild God of the world is sometimes merciful
    to those
That ask mercy, not often to the arrogant.
You do not know him, you communal people, or
    you have forgotten him;
Intemperate and savage, the hawk remembers him;
Beautiful and wild, the hawks, and men that are
    dying, remember him.

II

I'd sooner, except the penalties, kill a man than a
    hawk, but the great redtail
Had nothing left but unable misery
From the bone too shattered for mending, the wing
    that trailed under his talons when he moved.

*From Commission on English, *End-of-Year Examinations in English for College-Bound Students Grades 9-12* (Princeton, N.J.: College Entrance Examination Board, 1963), pp. 175-177. Used by permission of Joyce Miller Hodgins, CEEB Commission on English.

We had fed him six weeks, I gave him freedom,
He wandered over the foreland hill and returned in
    the evening, asking for death,
Not like a beggar, still eyed with the old
Implacable* arrogance**. I gave him the lead gift
    in the twilight. What fell was relaxed,
Owl-downy, soft feminine feathers; but what
Soared: the fierce rush: the night-herons by the
    flooded river cried fear at its rising
Before it was quite unsheathed from reality.

Directions:

Do the following work, using complete sentences for all answers.

1. Point out the significance for this poem of the plural in the title "Hurt Hawks."

2. Comment on each of the following words or phrases so as to show what it contributes to the effectiveness of the poem as a whole.

    (a) jags (line 1)
    (b) like a banner in defeat (line 3)
    (c) the lame feet of salvation (line 9)
    (d) the lead gift (line 35)
    (e) unsheathed from reality (line 40)

3. Describe the point of view of the poetic speaker (the "I" in the poem), showing how this point of view emerges and develops through implication and statement in the course of the poem. In doing this, you may want to consider not only what the poetic speaker says but the tone in which he says it.

4. This poem relies heavily on contrast for its effectiveness, as, for instance, when it contrasts the "communal people" and the hawk (lines 21-23). State two other important contrasts which you find in this poem, and show fully and specifically what each contributes to the effectivess of the poem as a whole.

Sample Answer. Score: High

Hurt Hawks is a poem of deeper significance than the mere death of a wild fowl. A hawk is a symbol of might, and arrogance, and freedom, of mastery and of a savage heart. Some men in dying are like hawks. They are powerful in their incapacity because they are chosen creatures of God. They are arrogant as they face an end which must come to all. This is a poem about the death of one hawk, but its meaning engulfs all of the strong and proud beings humbled and facing their ends. For that reason the poem has a plural title. The "hurt hawks" of the world are not only the wounded birds of prey but also the men who have been humbled from a position of greatness.

The author himself is a hawk, an arrogant, proud, and free man. He feels the power that he sees latent in the maimed animal which he has fed, only to have to shoot in the end. The author has a certain contempt, and yet pity, for the others

---

*implacable—not able to be appeased or pacified
**arrogance—unbearable pride; haughtiness; disdain

of his race who are not like the hawks, who do not know the God of beauty and wildness. He calls them "communal people", and says that if they did know such a God, they have forgotten him. Only dying men can recall his magnificence.

The author speaks too in sadness. He hated to kill the hawk, to see the creature maimed as it was. Yet he felt the fierceness of the spirit as it departed, leaving behind a body that was really only "soft feminine feathers." His sadness is a melancholy as he regrets the passing of wild beauty, and recalls how many of his fellow men lack the quality or ability to see it. Through the entire poem the author has expressed his respect and awe of this beauty and feeling of freedom and command. The closing lines express the author's conviction that such a spirit is never conquered even though the body which contained it is destroyed.

In line 1 "jags" is used to describe the bone which is broken, the supporting "pillar" of the wing. "Jags" suggests sharpness, thereby the feeling of pain, and the feeling of something strong emerging from a soft bloody mass. This emphasizes the power and significance of the wound, giving it dignity. Yet, "the wing trails like a banner in defeat." This image is used to convey the helplessness of the situation for the hawk. A banner is a symbol of conquest and pride, of excitement and movement. In defeat a banner sags, touches the ground, and can no longer fly freely in pride and pursuit. Such is the condition of a hawk with a broken wing. He can no longer fly proudly in attack and in arrogance.

"The lame feet of salvation" is used in line 8 to convey the idea that death, the final saving from pain, comes slowly and will not hurry. Death limps toward those who await it. Salvation will not move swiftly to the pent up creature who lives only for death to relieve his misery.

The hawk, even in his wounded condition, does not lose his characteristics of haughty pride and alertness. "The intrepid readiness" in line 17 signifies this constant alertness, fearlessness which must remain with predatory creatures. The hawk cannot be humbled by a wound. He is still the master.

"Unable misery" indicates that the hawk is helpless in his pain, and that his pain can be of no help to him. His wound cannot be healed, he is unable to do anything but wait and suffer. "The lead gift" of line 35 is the bullet which killed the hawk, which gave him the end he had so long awaited. "Lead" indicates heavy as well as metal: a heavy gift, a gift of sadness. The shot is a "gift" because it brings the death which is the only salvation for a dying hawk. "Unsheathed from reality" in the last line is again an image. The hawk's soul leaves his body to soar upward to live again in another world. It still has power and cannot be killed. Before the hawk quite died, before his soul was "unsheathed from reality" and had left his body, the night herons had been terrified as it flew upward across the sky. The same ability to inflict terror is in the soul, now "unsheathed from reality" as it leaves the soft, "owl-downy" feathers behind.

The author has used not only special phrases to convey his idea, but also has used various contrasts. The first contrast is of a wing jagging from "the clotted shoulder." This gives emphasis to the visual picture and mental image of the power of the wound. The contrast of "use" and "live" in line 4 emphasizes the idea of previous conceit and superiority, compared with the humbling to an existence of famine which the hawk undergoes. "Night" and "dawn" are contrasted in lines 9 and 11. Night and the dream world are splintered by dawn, daylight, and a light which reveals reality. The night was black and hid the pain and truth, but dawn brings the day which will not. "Communal people" are contrasted to the hawk because they do not know the hawk's god. This serves to point out again the arrogance of "hawks" and the discouraging state of those who do not know freedom and power. "Man" and "hawk" are contrasted again when the author says he'd "sooner . . . kill a man." This once again emphasizes the greater worth and power in a "hawk." Such contrasts can be found throughout the poem. The hawk came back "not like a beggar" and "what fell was relaxed, . . . but what soared: the fierce rush:" Through such use of contrasting words and images the poet conveyed his theme of the glory of a dying hawk, or a dying man.

Unique in its setup is this case study of a variety of ways in which students on the tenth grade level handled the same assignment. The author gives a brief insight into each student's background as well as the strengths and weaknesses of her paper. These themes, Miss Post hastens to add, were impromptu, written within a half-hour period. The author has managed to show each of the five themes in relation to the other four, dwelling on the "range of accomplishment" against the disparity of training each student writer had up to this point.

FIVE COMPOSITIONS FROM A TENTH GRADE COLLEGE PREPARATORY CLASSROOM*

WINIFRED POST

Offering a chance for a long, thoughtful look at the actual writing of students is a practical answer to the swelling chorus of minor key laments that English teachers are frittering away their time on frills, that their students can no longer write their own language, and that English composition is going either to the dogs or to pot — take your pick of these two charming destinations. The purpose of this article is to provide materials for just such a long, thoughtful look, using the half-hour composition assignment set by the Independent Schools Education Board on its January, 1961, Form D, examination in English and following it with five compositions written by students at the beginning of tenth grade at Dana Hall School in Wellesley, Massachusetts. A description of each student writer and an evaluation of her performance follow each composition.

THE QUESTION

Write a composition in which you develop an idea suggested by *one* of the following quotations. Even though your chosen quotation may lead you to tell a brief story or give various examples from your knowledge or experience, you should incorporate your story or examples in a composition which develops a point directly related to the quotation.

Your composition will be graded on (1) the organization of your material; (2) the degree to which the content deals with the quotation selected; and (3) the general mechanical competence of your writing.

1. " 'Tis with our judgment as our watches, none
    Goes just alike, yet each believes his own."
2. "A little learning is a dangerous thing."
3. ". . . fools rush in where angels fear to tread."
4. "To err is human, to forgive divine."
5. "Of all the causes which conspire to blind
    Man's every judgment and misguide the mind,
    What the weak head with strongest bias rules,
    Is Pride, the never failing vice of fools."

---

*Winifred Post, "Five Compositions from a College Preparatory Classroom," *Focus*, XIII (December 1962), pp. 13-16. Used by permission of Winifred L. Post.

SAMPLE 1

'Tis with our judgment as our watches, none
Goes just alike, yet each believes his own.

Have you ever had a new watch that just won't keep time? First it gains a little, then it loses even more time. It is annoying. When the watch is finally fixed it still may gain a minute a day or lose five minutes a week. This is inevitable, so you cope with it and do not bother to subtract thirty seconds when it says twelve o'clock.

Our judgement is the same type of problem. When we are young it cannot always be depended upon. A ten-year-old may not be trusted to drive a car, while a sixteen-year-old may not be trusted with alcoholic beverages. It is all a matter of experience and adjustments, as with the watch. We are not permitted to vote until we are twenty-one years of age. This is because our minds may still be running "five minutes slow or a minute fast." We may rush into judgements without considering all the available material, or we may be too lazy to think about things and simply close our eyes and pick an answer from the hat. With age and experience we are given opportunities to try our judgements and learn from the results, just as we try slowing down the watch a notch or speeding it up.

Yet with all these faults in judgement, we are all inclined to believe our own thoughts. "Why is this true?" you ask. It is a fairly simple idea. Going back to the watch we notice that it rarely keeps perfect time. So with our judgements we are rarely exactly right. Yet, we believe the watch, and when asked for the time, we give it in a loud, clear voice completely confident that we are correct. Our judgements have the same effect. We know that they may not be completely right, but they express our thoughts and conclusions, so we express them freely and loudly. Giving a judgement is as easy as giving time. It is being judged that becomes difficult, just as correcting the watch is often hard.

Each watch is a little different. It has different insides and a different face. Likewise each person is not identical to another. We are all different inside and have different figures, hair colors, and features. Our judgements emerge from our experiences and personalities. They are, therefore, slightly different also. We believe in them, because we believe in ourselves as God's children and as working machines that will not fail. Perhaps there is some irony here. We also believe in watches as working machines that will not fail. Is your judgement completely dependable?

The writer of the above composition entered the tenth grade at Dana Hall from a junior high school in Connecticut. She had written an excellent English test for admission to Dana Hall and came outfitted with a very high I.Q., and an all A record from her junior high school. For an impromptu essay written in the final half hour of a bristlingly difficult two-hour examination, this girl's performance is a bit of light in the murky landscape painted by those who claim that students can't write. Technically the writing is not flawless, but flawlessness seldom moves in partnership with the examination stop watch. The occasional *it* with a loose or vague referent, the comma dividing the two main clauses in the second sentence, the fondness for *yet* at the beginning of a sentence or even the beginning of a paragraph, are more than balanced by the general competence with language and the highly effective though deceptively unpretentious style that packs each sentence with meaning and with meaning highly relevant to the examination question. The organization of the paper is firm — unusually so for impromptu writing. Each new paragraph grows easily, naturally, inevitably out of the preceding paragraph. The student is in control of her material, riding it instead of letting it ride her. She knows where she is headed and she gets there. The reasoning proceeds almost wholly by analogy, and certainly the assignment invited the method. An older, more verbally sophisticated student might have been more conscious of the slipperiness of analogy and might have started her second paragraph with, "Our judgement is a *similar* type of problem" instead of "Our judgement is the *same* type of problem." And surely an older, more sophisticated student would have avoided the logical difficulties in the final sentence of paragraph three. Even so, much of the analogy in this composition operates persuasively and effectively; and with a student so obviously able, a composition like this opens the way for a conference on how analogy works in language and in logic and just where its dangers and difficulties lie. That this student fully grasps the quotation is obvious from the first sentence to the last. That she can move beyond the quotation to its implications and do so with mature perception is evident especially in the final paragraph which reaches a new depth of understanding that gives dignity and importance to the entire paper.

SAMPLE 2

A little learning is a dangerous thing.

Those who know a little about something often make more trouble than those who are ignorant of the subject. For instance, if a person has heard a little of treating injured people, he may try to help them in the wrong way. He may cause more damage to the injured person by treating him for the wrong thing. However, if someone who knows nothing of first aid finds someone hurt, he may immediately call a doctor instead of moving the person or trying to help. Thus the victim is helped more by an ignorant person than the one slightly skilled.

In a lighter vein, if someone knows a little on a certain subject, he may become more confused about it than if he knew nothing. From my own experience, I have run into this. In Math class we had to write a paper on *Zero*, and so we all ran out to find something about *zero* that nobody else knew. The more I thought about *zero* the more confused I became. The more I learned about it the more remote and indefinable *zero* became. It would be better to ask someone in the fifth grade what *zero* is because at that age you know *exactly* what it is.

Some people who know a little about something can become very boring and unbearable because they talk endlessly when they don't know what they're talking about! This is another example of small knowledge being more trouble than it is worth, to other people if not to the bore.

The saying "A little learning is a dangerous thing" is certainly true in many instances. If the whole world knew a little about everything it would be "talking through its hat" most of the time.

This student can also write. She entered our tenth grade from a private school in Delaware with a strong record, a high I.Q., and a highly competent English admissions test. The composition printed here was superior to most of the responses to this particular quotation mainly because she understood the quotation with the sharp precision of an able student, whereas less able people missed it either partly or wholly. Technically the writing is strong. This student doesn't make mistakes when she writes under pressure, although here, as in Sample 1, the style is not flawless. (Note the shift of person in the final sentence of paragraph two.) The organization is adequate and orderly but more perfunctory than that of Sample 1. Paragraph three could do with a smoothing transition to toll the reader on from paragraph two, and the opening sentence of the final paragraph is uninspired. The quality of the specific illustration, however, is an evident strength of this paper. The opening illustration is direct, concrete, forceful, and appropriate. The second demonstrates this student's resourceful use of her own experience. The touches of humor, as in the section on zero and in the final sentence, are further strengths in an already strong paper.

SAMPLE 3

A little learning is a dangerous thing.

To learn a lot is good for then you know and can make correct conclusions. If a man knows a lot about something he can draw conclusions of his own and understand this thing. He can make use of it and incorporate it into his life. But, if he knows only a little about this thing then he cannot make use of it. He will draw false conclusions on this subject, and, thinking he knows about it, may try to use the material in his work. It will cause him to make mistakes and err, and, not understanding it very well he may find himself telling falsehoods about it and making a fool of himself. If he knows a little he may get the wrong impression and this will hamper him. He may use this material incorrectly.

It is better to know nothing at all on such a subject. Then one cannot draw wrong conclusions or make mistakes concerning it. Certainly it is better to know nothing than very little about such a subject.

This student has far more ability than her composition reveals. She came to Dana Hall from a private school in Massachusetts. Her I.Q. is somewhat above our school's median of 120; she wrote a clearly acceptable admissions test in English and got a B in English at the end of the ninth grade in her previous school. Her evident understanding of the quotation from Pope is the great strength of an otherwise very modest performance. Technically the writing is decent, but the total output is too slight to afford much opportunity for achieving either errors or excellences. The glaring weakness is the lack of specific detail, the lack of illustrations, the refusal ever to move out of an enveloping fog of vagueness and generalities. The failure to pin down "something" in the second sentence, the later reference to the vague "something" as "this thing" or "it" and finally the speciously specific "this material" and "such a subject" indicate an acute case of the most common malady with which English teachers have to cope. The only cure is to go over the paper with the student, pointing out the vagueness, the lack of illustrations, the unbuttressed generalities, and letting her read other students' papers which do what she has failed to do. A student as intelligent as this one can learn. She has learned, and the result of the learning was a final examination rich in wisely used illustrative detail.

SAMPLE 4

A little learning is a dangerous thing.

Learning is a wonderful thing but often it can hurt someone. This happens every year in families. When a child learns there is no Santa Claus his whole Christmas is entirely ruined. I know my Christmas was destroyed, and I dread the day when my brother learns.

Friendships have often been split by merely learning a fact. Usually it is gossip, but that actually is a means of learning. I must admit it is a dangerous means.

Every year scientists discover new facts. Some are harmless, and others are extremely harmful. Eventually we will use some of our learned material, but the problem is that others will be destroyed.

We learn wonderful and beneficial things when we go to school. The time that we learn dangerous material is when we are with friends after school.

Religion is something we cannot learn too much about. God has hidden many facts from us. I am very glad because a way could easily start if we knew more than we should. I believe this is God's way.

I am not a fatalist, but when we learn dangerous things this could very well be a way God is developing us into better people. "A little learning is a dangerous thing,"—but often we learn something that God intended us to know.

This girl came from a private school in Massachusetts, with a respectable but unexciting English admissions test, a final grade of C in English at the end of the ninth grade in her previous school, and an I.Q. considerably below our school's median score of 120. In writing skills this composition is fairly decent for impromptu writing, though reference of pronouns is repeatedly dubious or vague. The main trouble is failure fully to understand the quotation. The opening paragraphs edge toward it but never quite get there. Nowhere does the student ever come to grips with the force of the all important adjective *little* in the phrase "a little learning." The organization of the material is haphazard and capricious. Paragraphs do not follow logically from their predecessors. The composition lacks unity. The reasoning is fogbound, especially in the last two paragraphs which bog down in sanctimonious inanities. Help for this kind of student must reckon first with her limitations. Even skillful teaching will never enable her to write like the author of Sample 1. She can learn, though, to make a simple, clear outline to give her compositions point and purpose, and she can learn to glue her paragraphs together with the verbal mucilage of transitions. In talking over this particular composition with her, one would first try to draw her attention to the key words "little" and "dangerous" in the quotation. Reading the work of abler students might also help unless the gap between them and her produced disheartened impotence on her part.

SAMPLE 5

A little learning is a dangerous thing.

> With out learning it is impossible to succeed. In this time it is even more imperative to be educated. When I say "educated," I don't fully mean learning what is taught in a book or what is taught at school, being educated by experience is just as important. One learns better by experience, unfortunately.
>
> A little learning is dangerous because you will not know where to start a problem or ambition with out knowledge of right and wrong. People could not live with out learning. To live with other people one must know to an extent what to do at times or where to go. One is always made to make a decision during a lifetime and that decision might alter the success or failure of the person. One could not even decide without education. Life is failure without education.

The writer of this composition prepared for Dana Hall at a junior high school in the suburbs of New York City. Her English admissions test for Dana Hall was weak; her final grade in English from her previous school was a C; and her I.Q. was far below the Dana Hall median. The composition printed above represents rock bottom performance from one moving about in worlds unrealized. Although the writing lacks any distinction, it is not abysmal. Most English teachers have seen worse. That, perhaps, is the most encouraging comment one can make about a student like this. The initial trouble is inability to understand the quotation. The writer of Sample 4 occasionally groped her way toward the target. This one merely gropes. Occasionally there is the germ of an idea, as in the second sentence of the first paragraph, and certainly her sentiments on the worth of education are unassailable; but unfortunately nothing of what gets said relates intelligibly to a quotation totally outside the student's grasp. This composition couples the vagueness of Sample 3 with the chaotic logic of Sample 4, and in so doing achieves a new low all its own. Her performance on this question is in line with a year of difficulty, discouragement, and setbacks, climaxed by an E (failure) on the final examination. For such a girl the answer is either another school or special sectioning with students whose abilities are not dishearteningly better than her own. With patience, understanding, and the right setting, such a girl can learn to write clear, correct, acceptable English at a simple level; but no teaching can turn her into a gifted writer. Even English teachers who wrestle daily with the impossible cannot pull off that miracle.

No one in his senses would dream of generalizing about the state of English on the basis of five compositions written under examination conditions in answer to a single question. Nevertheless the range of accomplishment represented here suggests the Johnsonian answer to those who say English teachers don't teach composition and students can't write: "Which teacher? Which student?"

The following themes illustrate (1) the unexpanded topic idea, (2) writing which grows from reading, and (3) creative handling of personal experience. Grades given by a large number of evaluators are surprisingly alike.

EVALUATING TWELFTH GRADE THEMES*

Illinois English Bulletin

RIVERS

Did you ever stop to think what a river was? A river is used for many things such as a home for the beaver and fish. They supply us with natural beauty like the Mississippi River as illustrated by the colorful writer Mark Twain. They are used as a source of transportation and of course in the days gone by the river boat.

There are rivers other than the Mississippi, such as the Wabash, the Missouri, the Red river, the Rio-Grande, the Arkansas, and the Kishwakee.

EVALUATION

	High school	College
Quality of content	Poor	Poor
Originality of treatment	Poor	Poor
Unity	Poor	Poor
Coherence	Poor	Poor
Emphasis	Poor	Poor
Paragraphing	Poor	Poor
Diction	Poor	Poor
Grammatical usage	Poor	Poor
Sentence structure	Poor	Poor
Spelling	Good	Good
Punctuation	Fair	Fair

Median grade given by high school teachers: E (17 E, 4 D); median grade given by college teachers: E (14 E)

COMMENTS TO THE STUDENT

With a flood of material available to you, you have produced a very meager theme. Haven't you had any personal experience with rivers? Don't you fish or swim? Haven't you gone sailing, or rowing, or canoeing?

Do you know well any river in this area? If so, you might like to tell about seeing it at a certain time, or at some season of the year. Do you know the history of this river, or any stories about its past?

Develop the second, third, and fourth sentences of the first paragraph into three separate paragraphs, and you will have a theme.

---

*From *Illinois English Bulletin*, 40, 7 (April 1953; reprinted March 1962), 7-8, 47-50, 25-27, 41-44. Used by permission of *Illinois English Bulletin*, Wilmer A. Lamar, Editor.

Thomas Hardy, the author, said Eustacia was the raw material of a divinity. She possessed the instincts and passions of a model goddess. Her striking appearance made a suitable background for the exotic desires she had. The wrath and fire of Eustacia's soul were balanced by a dignity and triumph in her bearing. Selfish, irresponsible, and discontented, Eustacia was used as a plaything of Destiny which was governed by love and passion. Entirely unfamiliar to her was a love such as Venn had for Thomasin: undemanding, free from the selfishness of his desires.

Fate introduced Clym Yeobright, an enchanting newcomer from the world Eustacia dreamed of, to the Heath. If Eustacia had been endowed with the gift of contentment know to Clym, she would have led an ordinary but worthwhile life. As she was, she disliked the near, liked the far, and was enchanted by the extraordinary. "Do I embrace a cloud of common fog?" were her words when Wildeve said he cared for her and would take her away from Egdon Heath. Eustacia realized her passion for Wildeve was a volatile thing. It was humiliating to have him when Thomasin no longer wanted him.

Fate had placed Eustacia not in her enchanting Paris, or even in Budmouth, but on lonely Egdon Heath. She hated the heath-folk and all man-kind. Clym once told her there was no use in hating human beings. Rather, she should hate what produced them. She replied, "Do you mean Nature? I hate her already." The Heath, loved dearly by Clym, was, to Eustacia, " . . . my cross, my shame, and will be my death."

Eustacia did not bother to rebel against human beings, for there were no figures on Egdon Heath important enough to incur her wrath. Mankind as a whole might have been blamed for her life on the Heath, but she felt Destiny was responsible for her unfortunate placing. Eustacia told Venn though there was a beauty in the Heath, it was a jail to her. She resigned herself to whatever was in store for her. She felt her actions were inconsequential and would have no bearing on a final outcome, so she lived with few cares and customs.

The loneliness of the heath and her hatred of it intensified her one desire; a consuming love. Her desire was not for any special lover but rather for one of such personality that she could be entirely absorbed by him; (if not for a lasting time, a brief romance would do). A passionate love, soon lost, was more desirable to Eustacia than a lifetime of congenial companionship.

The foreordained future, in Eustacia's mind, could not be altered. It would bring the passionate love of youth she desired and which would fade as time went on. Reality of the future was an element avoided by Eustacia: "I dread to think of anything beyond the present. What is, we know."

Since Eustacia's great desire for love was slow in coming to her, she turned to other fields of interest. Though she disliked the heath-folk, she associated with them to please herself. Eustacia told Clym she went mumming " . . . to get excitement and shake off depression." The cause of her depression was stated simply as "Life."

Eustacia was a pitiable figure. Her spirit was finally broken by her unhappiness. Though she had yearned to be a great woman, Destiny had dealt her a cruel blow by placing her in Egdon Heath. It was as if a judgment had been placed upon her, discernible to the heath-folk as well as to herself. At first she tried to " . . . look with indifference upon the cruel satires that Fate loves to indulge in," but this was finally changed to a bitter revolt against fate. Things beyond the control of mankind twist many good intentions. Whatever great dreams Eustacia might have had, Destiny had given her an unfortunate lot.

Your use of specific details to establish your points is good. But your them. "fuzzy" in purpose. When a theme is purposive and clear, all its paragra develop a single idea. What do you want your paragraphs to say about rive Make a sentence that contains the answer; then try writing paragraph to sentences that develop your theme sentence. Develop one of these senten in each paragraph.

Did you ever stop to think what an essay is? It is a chance to tell someon sensibly and clearly, something which he may not know, or which he may no have thought of in just the way that you think of it. It is not just a series of cas ual, half-shaped observations flung down haphazardly on the paper. It is an attempt to communicate something of interest and importance, not just the churn- ing out of one hundred words before Tuesday morning. If you think of essays as more than just busy-work, you will see why you must develop your points fully and connect them.

Comments to Teachers

This suggests to me that the writer just isn't capable of much connected think- ing. Try putting something into the jug before you try to get much out. Work first for the ideas. The form will follow.

This student needs to be shown the beauty of the commonplace. Suggest that he narrow his subject and restrict his writing to the things with which he is ac- quainted.

This pupil needs to be aware of the importance of selecting one controlling idea. He does not know how to gather details to support an idea. Through the analysis of a simple but well-written model he can be shown the effect of unity and organization. He should first learn to write a well-rounded paragraph.

Talk over with the student how Mark Twain treats the Mississippi River in his writing. Show the student how Twain made the description rich in facts. The student may be interested in rivers and would enjoy the discovery of the River Series.

This theme reflects the need for more theme writing, writing that will excite the imagination and move the intellect to express ideas.

If the assigned topic was just "Rivers," then I feel rather sympathetic with this boy — I'm sure he's a boy — for he is probably the type that would rather be on a river than writing about "rivers." You will have to catch his interest before he will give any time of his own or voluntary consideration to writing a theme.

Destiny's Displaced Person

Eustacia Vye possessed a beauty of color and limb that was unequalled by any woman around her. Her tall, straight figure was soft to the touch; her dark flaming eyes matched the glorious silken hair that crowned her head. Even in a more populated region than Egdon Heath, Eustacia's appearance would have been judged as striking.

EVALUATION

(Marked *Good* in all categories by both high school and college teachers) Median grade given by high school teachers: A (1 C, 2 B, 18 A); by college teachers: A (1 C, 4 B, 9 A)

COMMENTS TO THE STUDENT

You have exceptional ideas and exceptional sentence structure. You have made excellent use of quotations, showing a good understanding of the novel. Your opening and closing paragraphs are excellent.

Instead of using "so" as a connective between clauses, begin your sentence with a subordinate conjunction ("because") and omit the "so."

The chief way in which the sketch could have been made even better would have been by giving greater attention to the demands of coherence, by seeing to it that your statements flow naturally and clearly from sentence to sentence, from paragraph to paragraph. For instance, midway in the second paragraph, your series "selfish, irresponsible, and discontented" hits the reader with an excessively abrupt thud after your previous buildup of Eustacia.

This is a thoughtful study. The chief weakness is a tendency to break the unity of one section by admitting ideas inadequately discussed elsewhere. To avoid this, outline your compositions and put ideas in proper compartments.

COMMENTS TO TEACHERS

We find this sort of writing so rarely that most of us are inclined to overrate it when we do — we are so much impressed by *splendor formae* that we overlook the fact that the substance of the paper is almost entirely derivative. This student should be encouraged to expound his own conceptions, to work toward his own imaginative reconstruction of experience.

As a subject, offer some challenging questions that can't be answered just by repeating what the novel says, though quotations are acceptable when used to support a writer's opinion. I have made such a list of topics and questions for this novel and have used it with good results.

This student is so promising that a teacher ought to spend some time discussing with him some fairly subtle questions of coherence; e.g., should the material in paragraph three have been held until later in the theme? Equally, suitable choices in diction could profitably be discussed. In what sense, for example, does he use "matched" in the second sentence? In the seventh paragraph what does he mean by "reality of the future"? Finally, we must remember that even good writers are stimulated by compliment. I would compliment this writer for maintaining a pleasantly discursive tone, instead of the schematized enumeration of "traits" which often passes for a character sketch.

The author of this theme is evidently a lover of literature. She should be encouraged to *read* and to *write*. (She probably will become a teacher of English!)

WHY I CONSIDER "THE WORLD IS TOO MUCH
WITH US" A GREAT PIECE OF LITERATURE

What is a great piece of literature? Great writings have been found in all
periods of literature. The Romantic Age brought a "return to the exuberance,
the intensity, and mental independence of the Elizabethians." Surely a great
Romantic work should exemplify these ideals, and what could express them
more perfectly than William Wordsworth's sonnet, " The World is too Much
With Us"? First of all, there is a return to the exuberance when he tells of
the sea as she bares her bosom to the moon, of the howling winds, or perhaps imagine even old Proteus, or stately Triton rising from the sea and blow-
ing his pearly horn. The intensity of thought is apparent throughout the
entire sonnet; Wordsworth's excellent philosophy has been compiled in four-
teen exquisite lines. Nothing said is hypocritical; it has not delved too deeply
into the complex human mind. It is merely sage words of observance and wisdom. Nothing is said that is superfulous. Surely the mental independence is
obvious. Is not Wordsworth's philosophy unique? . . . After all, he is considered to be the "high priest of nature." Has he a literary superior who writes
with the same philosophy? He has not followed a pattern set by any of his
predecessors. He has set his own pattern of mental independence.

EVALUATION

	High school	College
Quality of content	Fair	Fair
Originality of treatment	Fair	Fair
Unity	Fair	Fair
Coherence	Fair	Poor
Emphasis	Fair	Fair
Paragraphing	Fair	Fair
Diction	Fair	Fair
Grammatical usage	Fair	Fair
Sentence structure	Fair	Fair
Spelling	Good	Good
Punctuation	Fair	Good

Median grade given by high school teachers: C (4 D, 13 C, 2 B, 2 A);
by college teachers: D (4 E, 4 D, 3 C, 2 B, 1 A)

COMMENTS TO THE STUDENT

How many ideas are in your theme? Then what should you do about paragraphing? A shorter title is usually preferable.

You have followed a definite plan in your theme and have presented in well-
selected words three ideas about Wordsworth's poem. This is commendable.
However, you should guard against assembling a mosaic of fragments from critical material which you have read without assimilating it thoroughly. It is much
better to try to express your own honest opinions in your own words and with
your own reasons.

Do you feel that you accomplished what you set out to do? You did not define
what you consider "great literature." You sidestepped when you characterized the

Romantic Age. You did convince me that the sonnet perhaps shows "exuberance," but from there on I was lost in a maze of words. What is really great about the poem? What shows its simplicity and its sincerity, two characteristics of great literature?

Your goal was to tell us why you consider this sonnet a great piece of literature. I feel that you have given us a critic's opinion rather than your own. Why do *you* think it is great? What has Wordsworth said to *you* that makes you feel it is great?

I'd like you to try a little experiment. Think of another sonnet by another Romantic poet, and then take this essay and see how many details and words you would have to change if you wanted this essay to fit the other poem. My guess is that you wouldn't have to make many changes. You see the trouble is that you are using language so loosely, both in your borrowing of the key words and in your interpretation of the poem, that no communication occurs. No relationship is established between the big general words and the reality of the poem.

Using the motto about exuberance, intensity, and independence is a good idea for starting the theme, and I can follow you pretty well through the exuberance, which you illustrate from the poem. But you neglect to tell us what it is in the poem that shows intensity, or where Wordsworth shows independence, or what it is that he shows independence of. And what philosophy appears in the poem?

COMMENTS TO TEACHERS

This student has been told to do something that he is not qualified to do; so he has done the next-best thing: hunted up an "authoritative statement" and tried to square the assignment with it. I would suggest that the teacher should give the students assignments which lie within his scope, instead of creating situations which virtually force him to use words irresponsibly.

In my opinion this is the least successful paper in the lot of twenty. In other papers which had to be graded down because of various failings in plan or execution, one could see the student groping to communicate something — some impression of rivers, newspaper office, or drugstore. One felt that the student, however fumbling in execution, had a toehold on reality. Here, however, the writer has cast off his moorings to reality. Handbook terms are using him, rather than he, them. This is not to say that this student may not become a much better writer than others in this group. Convince him that writing like this is nonsense, and he may be ready to begin learning.

The theme is mostly verbalism. Since the student is evidently not stupid, I assume that she (or he) learned somewhere that empty words are all that an English teacher cares about. That impression should be corrected! I suggest talking the poem over with the student, as well as the theme.

A better assignment would be "What the Poem X Means to Me."

The writer made the mistake of not answering "What is a great piece of literature?" and a further mistake of not applying the criteria (had he given them) to the sonnet. Students need to be taught to think straight. I realize that this is hard to do. But pin them down to explain the meaning of their high-sounding words.

My Darkest Hours

For weeks I had planned on taking my 4-H steer to the State Fair. Actually, it hadn't been weeks; it had been years, especially this last year. Finally it had narrowed down to months of training, feeding, currying, and watchful care, then weeks of preparation and now days weighted with anticipation.

I had been rushing around all day making a list of things I had to do, checking them off and adding others. When I paused for a moment, I glanced at my watch and saw it was time to feed my calves.

As I went down the feed-way aisle feeding my prizes, I was happily daydreaming about the fun I would be having in a few days. When I came to Chang, my best calf, I froze in horror at what I saw. His eye . . . his eye!

"Oh, no it just couldn't be! I must be seeing wrong for no *good* God would let such a thing happen!"

Instantaneously all of my years of dreams and hope shattered, for it looked as if Chang had been blinded in his right eye, the death blow to a show animal.

I tried to calm myself, but chills ran through me. I walked over, held Chang's head and made a closer observation. Weakly I groped for the railing, moving mechanically out into the evening breeze, and sank to the ground.

With Daddy and Mother away for the week I had no one to advise me on what to do. Pulling up snatches of grass, I sat trying to think, slowly coming out of my daze. I finally decided to go see a veterinarian living twenty miles away, who seemed to be the most confident. Although I doubted if Daddy would have readily consented, had he been there, I thought that would have been his final decision.

When I got to the veterinarian's all of the lights were out. It was only nine o'clock; surely he wouldn't be in bed already. Deafening howls from the vet's dog kennels began the minute I slammed the car door and increased in volume until by the time I reached the house, I half expected to be shot as a burglar.

I knocked and knocked but no one answered the door. Well, if he weren't home, I decided I'd wait until he came. At last I saw a light coming through the house. When the doctor answered the door I told him I thought Chang had snagged his eye on a nail or barbed wire. He said there was a very slim possibility that Chang could have snagged the tissue in his eyelid instead of the eyeball itself, and he would come the next day, for a staggering fee, and see what he could do.

The next evening as I watched the vet carefully inspect the injury I held my breath. It seemed to me that after I had waited and waited to know something, until it seemed impossible to stand the suspense, I found when the long awaited moment arrived, that I was afraid to learn the truth and would have preferred to wait a little longer.

After what seemed like hours he drew from his bag a dangerous looking instrument and deftly clipped away the eyelid tissue, which had been unexplainably torn.

All of my past hours of torture were ended in a split second, as quickly as they had begun, but I had lived a year in those hours.

EVALUATION

	High school	College
Quality of content	Good	Good
Originality of treatment	Good	Good
Unity	Good	Good
Coherence	Good	Good
Emphasis	Good	Good
Paragraphing	Good	Fair
Diction	Good	Fair
Grammatical usage	Good	Good
Sentence structure	Fair	Fair
Spelling	Good	Good
Punctuation	Fair	Fair

Median grade given by high school teachers: B (2 C, 11 B, 8A); by college teachers: B (5 C, 6 B, 3 A)

COMMENTS TO THE STUDENT

You kept me in suspense until I came to the last sentence. You made me realize how much work goes into producing a show animal for a State Fair. I am giving you a grade of A in spite of the fact that you have omitted some commas — but please be more careful next time. Correct the awkward expression that I have checked.

I can share your feeling. You have selected good details to present the feeling ("pulling up snatches of grass"). You plunged right into the narrative, kept us in suspense, and plunged right out — good. Would conversation add to the interest? You need to review paragraphing and revise yours. What is the effect of over-frequent paragraph divisions? Is your second sentence clear.

Some of your sentences are a bit awkward. Polish and perfect them in future compositions. Avoid extravagant expressions like "all my years of dreams and hopes," "my past hours of torture," "I had lived a year in those hours."

The beginning of the theme is slow — perhaps it could be shortened; the ending is hurried and requires filling out.

COMMENTS TO TEACHERS

Let the student grow by assigning provocative reading and letting him take part in discussing it.

This above-average paper raises a problem that most of us find peculiarly troublesome: What can we say to a student who, in narrating an event that has obviously moved him deeply, falls into clichés that threaten the effect he seeks? The student, deeply stirred, resorts to the stock language of cheap fiction or soap opera, and we get expressions like "I froze in horror" or ejaculations like "Oh, no it just couldn't be!" How can this tendency to pump up emotion be controlled without seeming to impugn the student's sincerity? I would not comment on these matters directly on the paper, since they are difficult to explain summarily, but in a conference I would try to thresh out the problem thoroughly, suggesting that hackneyed language, however forceful it may appear, cannot convey an impression of sincere feeling.

The main value of the essay samples in the Kentucky English Bulletin, *a publication of the Kentucky Association of Teachers of English, is the detailed analysis of two types of grading used for the same theme. In the first type, too much attention is given to mechanics; the second deals more with the writer's purpose and the tone of the comments is one of encouragement. Two other themes in this section have the added attraction of being graded by large numbers of evaluators who are in surprising agreement.*

TWO TYPES OF GRADING*

Kentucky English Bulletin

Too many errors. There are others which I could have marked.

you fail to stick to your subject

D

Grading to Identify and Correct Mechanical Errors

I Have Learned That the Swiftest Traveler Is He That Goes Afoot

℗ Most people today would say that traveling afoot is not a good way to travel. Perhaps for them that is right but if they only realized it, they have to depend upon someone else if they travel in any other manner.

agr. Traveling afoot a person can start when they please and stop when they please. You may find an interesting place and decide to stay for a while, being afoot and no one else to worry about, getting a job perhaps to have a little

awk. income while in this place. When you have settled your curosity you can move on with out any interfereance from anyone.

Being afoot you will probably travel very slowly, therefore getting more

Inc. sent. enjoyment out of the scenery. A large town, beautiful rugged mountains, cool stream and waterfalls, or anything that has any artistic beauty in it. Each or any of those may keep you fascinated for several days or week if you are alone on foot, whereas if you were with someone traveling otherwise you might not ℗ even stop to admire their beauty for even one day.

---

*From **Principles and Standards in Composition**, Kentucky English Bulletin, 6, 1 (Fall 1956). 318-323, 331-333, 337-339. Used by permission of W. S. Ward, Editor.

Ref; Someone may tell you that you can travel with <u>them</u> on a trip, but it may be

Ref. ten years before <u>they</u> decide to make the trip. Also with someone else there

agr. *where* <u>is</u> always split decisions on places to go, when to go, how to go, and many other

situations that one person has to face but just has himself to convince on

awk. how he is to go about the trip. He can always change his mind without <u>herting</u> *sp.*
P
anyone else's feeling's also if he is alone and afoot.

The greatest reason for traveling afoot being the fastest method of

P travel is: You do not have to wait on **any** man, It does not require the

P assistance of any mechanical object, generally the man who travels afoot can

have

start any day and not <del>having</del> to worry about what he has left behind.

Be more careful with your proofreading.

Your paper contains' all sorts of errors, but I see in it much promise also. Let's have a conference soon!

Do you really prove that travelling afoot has anything to do with speed? What thesis statement have you really developed?

D

Grading to
Teach Writing
and Thinking

I Have Learned That the <u>Swiftest Traveler Is He That Goes Afoot</u>

What is the normal punct. of a compound sent.?

Most people today would say that traveling afoot is not a good way to tra-vel. Perhaps for them that is right but if they only realized it, they have to depend upon someone else if they travel in any other manner.

Re-read your theme and see how often you shift back and forth between 3rd and 2nd person.

Traveling afoot a (person) can start when they please and stop when they please. (You) may find an interesting place and decide to stay for a while, being afoot and no one else to worry about, getting a job perhaps to have a little income while in this place. When you have settled your <u>curosity</u> *sp.* you can move on with out any <u>interfereance</u> *sp* from anyone.

Commas follow introd. elements containing verbs

Tense

Being afoot you will probably travel <del>very slowly</del>, therefore getting more
enjoyment out of the scenery. (A large town)(beautiful rugged mountains)(cool
stream and waterfalls)(or anything that has any artistic beauty) in it. Each
or any of these may keep you fascinated <del>for</del> several days or week, if you are
alone on foot, whereas if you <u>were</u> with someone traveling <del>otherwise</del> you might

You have four subjects but where is their verb?

not even stop to admire their beauty for even one day.

Someone may tell you that you can travel with them on a trip, but it may be ten years before they decide to make the trip. Also with someone else there is always split decisions on, places to go, when to go, how to go, and many other situations that one person has to face but just has himself to convince on how he is to go about the trip. He can always change his mind *Did you proofread?* without *herting* anyone else's feeling(g's) also if he is alone and afoot. *sp*

The greatest reason for traveling afoot being the fastest method of travel *Do you know what a comma fault is?* is: You do not have to wait on any man, It does not require the assistance of any mechanical object, generally the man who travels afoot can start any day and not having to worry about what he has left behind.

1. Your paper is based on a good idea and has a recognizable organization. Par. 1 states your over-all purpose; pars. 2, 3, 4 develop three reasons to support par. 1; par 5 is a recapitulation of 2, 3, 4. See if you can restate the topic sentence in each par. more clearly so as to make the steps in your progress more unmistakable.

2. See if you can find examples of faulty agreement in sent. 1 of par 2, and sent. 2 of par. 4.

3. Sent. 2 of par. 1 and sent. 2 of par. 4 are so garbled that the reader must reread and finally guess at their full meaning and purpose. See if you can improve them.

The first of these methods of theme grading — that of identifying and correcting mechanical errors — is valuable but is inadequate alone. It is the second method — the combination of marginal notations and terminal comments — that the compilers of this booklet advocate as a method which is both practicable and effective. In the first set of corrections the grader has conscientiously marked every error in spelling, punctuation, and grammar that he could find. When the student gets his theme back, however, he may feel quite discouraged, for the clipped abbreviations and symbols, the machine-like, impersonal tone has told him only that he has done poorly. The second grader, on the other hand, has read the composition carefully enough to discover the writer's purpose and plan and to appraise his successes as well as his failures. Furthermore, he has taken the time to formulate comments designed to help the author understand his faults and to correct them. As with the first correction, the student's errors have been marked, the grade is still a D, but there is a significant difference in the tone of the two sets of corrections. In short, there is no escaping the fact that the most important thing about the grading of papers is not the grade which a student receives, or even the marginal notations, but instead the critical comments, the constructive suggestions, and the encouraging words which the teacher writes on the paper when he places a grade on it or which he says to the student later in conference.

THE RETURNING OF THEMES

Theme Revision: When a student has his paper returned to him, he should be required to revise it so that he may receive full value from his writing experience. This revision may vary all the way from minor corrections on a superior paper to a complete rewriting of a paper that is poor in organization or that fails to give meaning to generalizations through the use of concrete particulars.

Conferences: Conferences are designed to help individual students with their personal writing problems as distinct from the general difficulties which many in the class share and which therefore should be taken up in class. With some students much of the time will be given over to mechanics, but it is important that the teacher reveal his concern with what the student is trying to say. It is important that the student come to value his teacher as a sympathetic, if critical, reader who expects themes to be individual and interesting. Otherwise the student is likely to think of his conferences as help sessions on punctuation and his themes as routine sets of grammatical sequences properly punctuated. This is not to say that a teacher will have spent his conference time unwisely if much of it is devoted to mechanics, but ordinarily he will have done better if he shows the student how he failed to limit his subject, define his terms, arrange his materials well, or develop an idea convincingly; how honest exposition is the fair consideration of evidence, not the defence of biased opinion; and so on.

It should be understood, of course, that conferences are not for weak students only. The superior student and the average student as well should receive profit: the latter can be shown how his C paper lacks something; the former can be stimulated by having his instructor explore the implications of his papers, suggest thought-provoking topics for future writing, recommend books that he might find interesting; and so on. If a superior student leaves a conference with the feeling that he has done nothing more than have a little chat, or if the conference fails to get beyond grammar and mechanics, the instructor has probably been at fault. The well-planned conference does orally what the combination of marginal and terminal comment described above does in writing. It seeks to relate the student's weaknesses and strengths to the overall intention of his theme and thus to foster in him a greater insight into his writing problems.

CONCLUSION

In some schools — both high school and college — the procedures set forth in the preceding pages are likely to be regarded as above immediate attainment. The fact remains, however, that though the objectives may seem somewhat ideal to many, they have already been achieved in many schools and can be achieved with relative ease by many others; and they must be achieved by all if our graduates are to be able to express themselves with reasonable clarity and correctness. As has been pointed out already, any student or any school will be better off for having striven toward these objectives.

The number of compositions which a student writes during a year need not be great, but the teaching that goes into each one needs to be thorough. This does not mean, of course, that there can be no written assignments except under the near-ideal conditions just described. There should be. Short impromptu themes, an essay type of examination, any sort of writing that gives practice will also give fluency and confidence and thus is greatly to be desired. But beyond these kinds of writing must be the kind that is done under conditions approximating those described in the foregoing pages.

Themes, Analyses, and Comments

Notes on Grades and Analyses to Follow

A paper is no more graded in a vacuum than it is written in a vacuum. Hence grades and comments occasionally reflect the fact that a particular error is especially obnoxious to one teacher and hence draws a sharp penalty, whereas to another teacher, less offended by the defect in question, the merits of the same theme may seem rather impressive. It is probably impossible, therefore, to set forth — and even more difficult to apply objectively — criteria and standards that will enable all who read to agree immediately on the grade which a theme should receive.

Despite individual differences and the inevitable necessity for subjective judgments, however, the grades and comments of those who have participated in the preparation of this booklet are notable for their agreement. With hardly an exception there is either a concentration on one grade or else a near-equal division between two contiguous grades. It is worthy of comment also that the evaluations by high school and college teachers coincide to a remarkable degree. There seem to be slightly higher standards among the college teachers, but the rise between high school and college is probably about the same as for each grade in high school.

The reader is reminded also that he is to assume that the themes were written by students just as they were graduating from high school or just as they were entering college, and that the grades were given and the comments prepared with such students in mind.

Finally, the letter system of grading (A, B, C, D, E), though widely used in Kentucky schools, may be translated for those not familiar with it as follows: A, superior; B, good; C, average; D, poor but passing; E, failing.

Theme 5   Grade Distribution
Rated A   A = 27
                                                             B = 14
                                                             C = 5
                                                             D = 0
                                                             E = 0

SPRING

Spring is a combination of many things. It is the brightness of the sun as it floods the world with its indispensable light. It is the moon rising like a huge red ball which later changes to yellow and pours its soft light over the quiet earth. It is sudden showers and strong winds, fleecy clouds and blue skies. Spring is melted snow and ice and swollen streams which cause devastating floods. Spring is the reappearance of familiar birds — the modest little wrens, the brilliant cardinals, the cheerful robins, the quiet blue birds, and the ostentatious blue jays. It is also the industrious "measuring worm" methodically and patiently measuring the slender new blades of grass or perhaps the dead, dry stalks of one of last year's weeds. Spring is a turtle coming out of the mud to sun himself on the bank of a pond; it is a chorus of frogs in the evening. It is the chattering squirrel as it noisily eats its diminishing supply of nuts and completes its meal by robbing a tree of the soft, new leaf buds. Spring is the redbud and dogwood trees displaying their brilliant colors; but even before these, it is the golden blossoms of the forsythia bushes. It is the dandelion-dotted lawns or the grass-dotted dandelion patches. Spring is little boys eagerly digging for fishing worms and going wading in forbidden creeks. It is the old farmer plodding along resolutely behind his plow and strong white horses. It is the young couple strolling hand-in-hand along the road side. Spring is the eager sun bathers, each one trying to get a darker tan than the others. Spring is jumping rope, shooting marbles, and playing softball games. Spring is a feeling — the joy of living, seeing, and learning. The combination of all of these things, and many more, makes up Spring as we know it.

COMMENT

In *Spring* the aim is to suggest the emotional quality of a season by an enumeration of carefully chosen and arranged details. All of the details are concerned with the notion of renewed vitality and thus prepare the reader to accept the concluding generalization that Spring is a feeling — "the joy of living, seeing, and learning." The paper's excellence is further accounted for by the emphasis put on arrangement, an emphasis which appears on the sentence level in the consistently used device of parallelism, in the grouping of sentences with related details, and in the over-all inductive framework. Within the framework there is a time-honored progression (used, for example, in the opening lines of the *Canterbury Tales*) beginning with weather phenomena, going on to the behavior of wildlife, and concluding with human activities. The technique verges on the poetic, particularly in sentences 2-5, where the controlling image of water, though not directly mentioned until sentence 4, is anticipated in the earlier sentences by the sun which *"floods* the world" and the moon which *"pours* its soft light"* on the earth.

There is room for improvement here, though not a great deal. The last sentence does little more than repeat the first, and both sentences seem external to the real development, which reaches its conclusion in the next to last sentence. The writer might consider omitting them altogether. Would paragraph indentations be helpful to mark the sentence groupings? Undoubtedly, as the theme now stands. However, at least as good a device would be to regularize the use of the subjects "Spring" and "It," so that "Spring" would occur only in the opening sentence of each group and "It" in the remaining sentences. Perhaps, too, a case can be made for moving sentences 10 and 11 (on trees and flowers) to a place following the opening "weather" section (sentences 2-5) as giving a more "natural" progression: weather, vegetable life, animal life, human life.

Finally, it might be remarked that theme topics such as this often lead to unfortunate results. That is to say, a less skillful writer may fail to exercise restraint and hence may attempt a pseudo-poetic, inflated style that is very objectionable to a mature reader. Even the present writer (in her use of cliches like "modest wrens," "cheerful robins," and "chattering squirrels") comes dangerously close to this fault at times.

Theme 8	Grade Distribution
Rated A	A = 32
	B = 12
	C = 3
	D = 0
	E = 0

I Was Scared

It all began one morning in early October, 1950. Tired men, dirty and short tempered, climbed aboard the convoy trucks they had loaded during the previous night. The convoy rolled at eight o'clock; everyone, including myself, felt better because it was our first time to relax in three days.

The morning, like most October days, was cool and refreshing, and most of us slept, at least until the sun rose high enough to make it miserably hot and impossible to relax. As we passed through the ravaged and bombed out cities, I had mixed feelings toward the people we saw there, a feeling of pity and a feeling of hate.

Soon we left the little villages behind and began climbing into the mountains where signs of human life are not seen for long intervals of time. Everything was quiet except for the rumble of heavy trucks and a lonely GI singing, "Carry Me Back to Old Virginia."

Even in Chosen the mountains are pretty this time of year with the leaves turning all colors and falling to the earth, blanketing it with beauty that cannot be described, only felt deep inside.

Yes, everything was quiet and peaceful until up ahead came the chatter of machine guns and the occasional crack of a Garand. I began to feel a little nervous and scared, no not scared, at least not yet. You see, it was my first experience with war. Our truck was the last in a long line, and as we were descending into a small valley, the brakes became hot and began to freeze.

We knew we would have to break convoy. There was a bombed out bridge at the base of the hill; we had to go around it and through a small creek: here is where it all began and nearly ended. When the truck reached the creek, the brakes were so hot we could not climb out of the embankment. The rear guard came by and asked if we needed assistance, which we declined because the only thing to do was wait for the brakes to cool.

The rest of the convoy went on, and we waited there, expecting to catch them later. There were five of us. While we were waiting, the chatter of guns could still be heard in the far off mountains — cleaning up, they called it, and that should explain itself since the front lines had moved on farther north.

A guy starts thinking when he is in a spot like that, and I was doing my share of it. A buddy just handed me a cigarette, when all hell broke loose. Bullets riddled the cab of our truck, and the chatter of machine gun fire roared in our ears. We hit the dirt or, I should say, hit the mud of the creek bed. Yes, I was scared. There we were, five guys alone in a small creek facing a Red machine gun and an unknown number of men. Yes, I was scared, plenty damned scared, and even worse than that, I knew of nothing to relieve the situation; but I wasn't alone.

We all said a silent prayer and thanked God that our little friends were such lousy shots. I often wondered how a greenhorn would feel with his first taste of war: then I knew. Only a few seconds had passed, yet it seemed like a life-time. Then, as suddenly as it began, the firing stopped. I could still hear the chattering of those guns and splattering of lead. It pounded in my head as though they were still firing. One of the guys yelled something; at first it didn't register, and then I looked up the road we had just come over; that column of dust was the loveliest thing I had ever seen.

The Convoy had been only a few minutes behind us. Their lead jeep, with a machine gun mounted in its cab, came roaring down the hill spitting out death. By this time the Reds had disappeared.

We had been initiated into the ranks of those who knew what it meant to be afraid. There was no shame because of our fear; we had discovered a new meaning for the word and silently agreed to respect it in its own right.

COMMENT

I *Was Scared* has what appears to be one of the simplest of all plans of organization, that of natural time order. This order alone, however, is not enough to guarantee an effective story or incident, for problems of selection and arrangement arise within any kind of general framework. The writer has solved these problems with considerable success by selecting details which chart not only the progress of the convoy but also the shifting moods of the men involved. Thus the movement is from the feeling of relaxation engendered by the quiet and beauty of the October morning as the convoy moves into the foothills, to the nervous tension aroused by the distant rifle fire and the trouble with the brakes of the truck during the descent into the valley, then to the paralyzing fear when the attack occurs in the creek bed, and finally when the second convoy brings relief, to the sober realization of the new meaning for the word "fear." The style ably supports the aim — which is to tell the truth simply and vividly without the varnish of false heroics; it abounds with sharply phrased details like "the occasional crack of a Garand," "the splattering of lead," and with the idioms of natural speech — "you see," "cleaning up, they called it," "a guy starts thinking," "plenty damned scared." It is clear that this writer is unusually mature: he knows how to grasp his own experiences and give them significant shape.

The faults are faults of detail only. The writer should be asked whether anything is gained by making the very specific reference to the *time* of the incident in the first sentence and withholding the *place* till paragraph 4. His attention should be called also to the way the tenses of the second sentences of paragraphs 7 and 8 (past instead of past perfect) work against the basic time order of the events he is relating. He should clear up such small matters as the incorrectly used reflexive ("including *myself*") in sentence 3 of paragraph 1; the cliche "spitting out death" in paragraph 9; and the needless comma before the song title in paragraph 3. Lastly, he should understand the reader's bewilderment to learn at the start of paragraph 9 that "The convoy had been only a few minutes behind us." Since only one convoy, the writer's own, has so far been mentioned, more explanation is needed at this point. Preparation for the rescuing convoy might be made in the first paragraph without destroying suspense, simply by revising the third sentence to "Our convoy, the first of two, rolled at eight o'clock . . . ."

From California comes this outline of norms and their application to six separate themes sans the regular grade marking. The authors are intent on applying standards to content, organization and style. In addition to their criticism of each essay, they have added qualities which teachers might expect to find in other essays written at about the same level. They note, finally, that while the scale was intended primarily for teachers, students might learn to use it profitably, also.

CALIFORNIA ESSAY SCALE[*]

California Association of Teachers of English

Section IV: Use of the Essay Scale

The following essay scale consists of an outline of criteria for the evaluation of compositions, a list of symbols used in the scale, essays representing five levels of quality, and pertinent critical comments.

The evaluation outline, which is the basis upon which the essays in the scale were judged, is necessarily short and obviously very general. It is intended simply as a guide, a reminder of the qualities which distinguish superior composition. In preparing such a guide the subcommittee found it impossible to define or to give examples of all terms employed, for to do so would entail the writing of a complete textbook on composition. Thus the teacher who attempts to use the outline in the evaluation of student papers must still decide, for example, whether ideas under consideration are relevant and well developed and whether vocabulary is accurate; for clearly enough, no definite answers to these questions can be given. The subcommittee suggests, however, that teachers who keep the outline in mind as they study the scaled essays and critical comments will find some assistance with these problems.

The symbols used in the scale are generally markings familiar to every trained teacher of English. They may be found fully discussed in standard handbooks of composition.

The five essays in the scale are reproduced word for word and error for error, just as the students wrote them, and arranged in order of quality from best to worst. The subcommittee, however, has made certain additions within the body of each selection: the sentences have been numbered to facilitate the observation of references made in the critical comments that follow, and italics and brackets have been added to direct attention to certain word groups commented on in the marginalia. (No student writer used either brackets or italics in his essay.) Proofreader's markings in the margins refer to errors near the margins in which the notations appear. Other marginal entries are self-explanatory. The subcommittee has attempted to mark the essays closely without being puristic.

[*]From California Association of Teachers of English, *A Scale for Evaluation of High School Student Essays* (Champaign, Ill.: National Council of Teachers of English, 1960), pp. 11-28. Used by permission of N. Field Winn, Chairman, Committee on Composition, California State Articulation Conference.

It should be noted, however, that markings are for the teacher's information; they would not necessarily be the same on essays which are to be returned to students. A few minor errors have been intentionally overlooked.

The critical comment accompanying each essay is an attempt to employ the general criteria of the evaluation outline in judging the quality of composition represented. It does not attempt to treat every item in the outline, for it seems pointless to discuss effective sentence structure, for example, in connection with a paper which illustrates a fundamental ignorance of the English language. Nevertheless, each critical comment seeks to illuminate the characteristic excellence and inadequacy of the paper under consideration, and in appropriate context, to offer some specific examples. Following each critical comment is a summary of qualities which may be expected in other essays at the same level.

The application of the essay scale, of course, will require judgment and some knowledge of composition. It is not a magic formula for the instructor who lacks adequate background in English, nor will it prove useful in the hands of a very weak student. The entire study was undertaken primarily for teachers, not for students. Nevertheless, adequate discussion of the scale and carefully guided instruction in its use should prepare the more conscientious high school seniors to employ it profitably in the evaluation of their own compositions.

The majority of teachers, however, will find the scale useful as a basis for departmental discussions of composition standards and grading policies, and the individual teacher may use it to determine areas of instruction requiring emphasis and to guide him in the marking of student papers. If the essays in the scale are used as a guide in grading, the teacher should remember that a good essay need not be without errors. Essay I in the scale has more errors noted than either Essay II or III; however, the more extensive development of the thought in Essay I and the manner in which it meets the standards of the evaluation outline result in a paper of better overall quality than either Essay II or III. Obviously some errors detract more from effectiveness than do others: for example, fragments, comma splices, faulty agreement of subject and verb, faulty pronoun reference, absence of proper transitions, and confused sentence structure. But the presence of a very few of these errors should not lead the teacher to regard an essay as a failure if the writer has expressed himself clearly and logically and has adequately developed a central idea.

For the teacher's use in evaluating an essay on a five-point grading system, the subcommittee suggests that Essay I in the scale might very well be considered an A, Essay II a B, Essay III a high C, Essay IV a low C, and Essay V a D. In his evaluation of essays the teacher will find it impossible to avoid subjective judgments, but despite this problem, he should remember always that he is grading composition; he is not grading the student's family background, interests, or personality.

Every student writer, the subcommittee believes, should be encouraged by appropriate marks and comments, but a student who does not write well should not be told that his accomplishment is creditable when it does not compare favorably with the acceptable essays in the scale.

SECTION V: THE EVALUATION OF ESSAYS

   I. Content: Is the conception clear, accurate, and complete?
     A. Does the student discuss the subject intelligently?
       1. Does he seem to have an adequate knowledge of his subject?
       2. Does he avoid errors in logic?
     B. Does the essay offer evidence in support of generalization?
   II. Organization: Is the method of presentation clear, effective, and interesting?
     A. Is it possible to state clearly the central idea of the essay?
     B. Is the central idea of the paper as a whole sufficiently developed through the use of details and examples?
     C. Are the individual paragraphs sufficiently developed?
     D. Are all the ideas of the essay relevant?
     E. Are the ideas developed in logical order?
       1. Are the paragraphs placed in natural and logical sequence within the whole?
       2. Are the sentences placed in natural and logical sequence within the paragraphs?
     F. Are the transitions adequate?
     G. Are ideas given the emphasis required by their importance?
     H. Is the point of view consistent and appropriate?
  III. Style and Mechanics: Does the esssay observe standards of style and mechanics generally accepted by educated writers?
     A. Are the sentences clear, idiomatic, and gramatically correct? (For example, are they reasonably free of fragments, run-on sentences, comma splices, faulty parallel structure, mixed constructions, dangling modifiers, and errors of agreement, case, and verb forms?)
     B. Is the sentence structure effective?
       1. Is there appropriate variety in sentence structure?
       2. Are uses of subordination and coordination appropriate?
     C. Is conventional punctuation followed?
     D. Is the spelling generally correct?
     E. Is the vocabulary accurate, judicious, and sufficiently varied?

SECTION VI: SYMBOLS USED IN MARKING THE ESSAYS

agr	agreement	p	punctuation
cap	capitals	red	redundant
cs	comma splice	ref	reference
d	diction	rep	repetitious
fc	faulty comparison	sp	spelling
frag	fragment	str	sentence structure
gr	grammar	t	tense
mm	misplaced modifier	trans	transition (needed)
o	remove punctuation (usually comma)	x	obvious error
pl	plural	//str	parallelism
pv	point of view	v	insert word
pred	predication	( )	make one word

SECTION VII: THE ESSAY SCALE

Essay I

Can It!

"which can be applied"

(1) "Swinus Americanus" is a name [often] applied to those <u>ignorant</u>   *d, "careless"* campers and travelers who find it easier to leave their refuse for someone else to pick up rather than dispose of it properly themselves. (2) A lack of

trans. (2) to (3)

outdoor manners is one of the primary reasons why people unconsciously destroy the natural beauty of our great out-of-doors. (3) The sum of money spent each year by local, state, and federal agencies to keep American clean

is almost unimaginable. (4) In Yellowstone Park, one of our largest tourist attractions, [it costs the U.S. government] over two million dollars a year to keep the roads and campgrounds free from trash and refuse.

(5) After the turn of the century, many prominent organizations, such as

cap. sp.

the Izaak Walton <u>legue,</u> realized the need of educating the element which dis-regarded all ethics of good camping. (6) Apparently, little progress was

preferably omitted

comma preferable

made, and the situation grew worse and worse. (7) In 1950, most of our *preferably omitted* highways and campgrounds looked like one huge trash dump. (8) Reform was

(8) Good emphasis

long overdue. (9) Up sprang a number of campaigns which stressed the importance of good outdoor manners. (10) The Keep America Beautiful Campaign was organized, and "litterbug" became a household word. (11) Municipal and state governments [joined the parade] by enacting laws which   *d* imposed heavy fines for careless motorists who littered highways and byways. (12) Magazines and newspapers carried articles ‸ and pictures of this shame-   *"about"* ful aspect of American life. (13) Little by little, the people grew aware of

(14) and (15) wandering

their responsibility of preserving what belonged to them. (14) "Preserving"

str: meaningless condition

is an accurate word [if one realizes] that campgrounds strewn with garbage

and disconnected

and litter are excellent breeding places for disease-bearing insects. (15) A piece of broken glass may magnify the sun's rays just enough to kindle a

fire which may envelop thousands and thousands of acres of valuable watershed.

(16) Cooperation with this clean-up campaign has been over-whelming.

sp,

(17) The manufactures of canned and bottled beverages are experimenting

agv.

with disposable paper or cardboard containers. (18) Gas stations have

volunteered to dispose of refuse-filled paper sacks which motorists carry

on their outings and replace this with a new sack. (19) In many parks, refuse

cans bear the insignia of an imaginary kangaroo called Parky. (20) ["Parky *not sufficiently developed*

says--"] is another familiar antilitterbug slogan. (21) Gradually, through

posters, pamphlets, articles, signboards, and emphatic speeches, Americans

have learned a valuable lesson in good manners. (22) The fight, however,

must continue. (23) Not until our roadsides, campgrounds, and parks appear

good unifying device

as they did before the advent of ["swinus Americanus"] will the fight be won. *comma preferable*

(24) By adhering to good outdoor manners, we will help to win this fight.

Essay I — Critical Comment

Though far from perfect, this essay is of sufficiently high caliber to illustrate the top of the scale. Its principal merits are its brisk, lively, well-cadenced style and its excellent use of concrete illustrative language. For example, in sentences 4 and 5 a less accomplished writer would have stopped at the comparatively vague "many prominent organizations" without adding the reference to the Izaak Walton League. (I) The essay is clear in conception and execution. (II) The organization of ideas is logical and coherent, proceeding from a general introductory statement of the importance of the problem to an analysis of steps taken and to be taken to improve the situation. Generally, the sequence of statements is clear and natural, although there are some lapses: sentences 14 and 15, for example, are not perfectly integrated into the paragraph. The whole paper has unity and completeness. It presents the central idea that although many natural beauty spots are being destroyed by careless campers, a concentrated campaign is making definite progress toward educating the public in outdoor manners. This idea is developed through such examples as the Izaak Walton League, the Keep America Beautiful Campaign, and cooperation of the gas stations. The paper is well rounded off by the last three sentences, which are conclusive without being repetitious. (III) Sentence structure is not always accurate (the first sentence confuses idioms of comparison; the syntax of sentence 14 is meaningless), but it is usually correct and effective; sentences 5 to 13 show a good and meaningful variety of constructions rhetorically effective. The only grammatical error of any seriousness is the agreement error of *this* in sentence 18.

●●●●●●

Essays in the first level of the scale are usually characterized by lively intelligence: the writer's thought flows easily from one idea to another; it grasps and expresses relationships among ideas and between abstract ideas and concrete realities. Sentence structure is usually both fluent and complex, vocabulary is extensive, and spelling is good. Such essays characteristically have excellent content, are frequently rather long, and have fully developed paragraphs. These qualities seem natural to a good mind. A young person's mind, however, may be somewhat undisciplined; thus the usual faults of essays in this range are in vocabulary, which, being ambitious, is sometimes experimental, and in organization and sentence structure, which may occasionally become a trifle confused. The quality of punctuation seems to vary considerably among the best papers.

Essay II

Juvenile Delinquency

(1) What are the real causes of juvenile delinquency? (2) Who is to blame for the misdemeanors of today's teenagers? (3) A few weeks ago, as one of a number of students representing the various high schools in Sonoma County, I was brought face to face with this problem of juvenile delinquency. (4) At the invitation of the County Probation Department, we attended a session of Juvenile Court and visited the County Jail and Juvenile Hall. (5) We had all been aware of the problem of criminal activities among minors, but after the tour, and especially after lengthy discussions with the supervisor of Juvenile Hall and with Mr. Becklund, County Probation Officer, we began to realize the full scope and gravity of the situation.

(6) Why, we asked, is juvenile delinquency such a problem? (7) Who is to blame? (8) "Parents," was the answer every time. (9) The teenagers we saw in Juvenile Court and in Juvenile Hall were there for many reasons, to be sure. (10) But all these stemmed from the same source--parents. (11) With some, it was lack of proper parental supervision; with some, a lack of one or both parents; and with others, neglect, disinterest, or depravity on the part of the parents. (12) There were, as in every case, a few exceptions to this generalization. (13) What about those offenders whose excuse was rebellion against conformity, against the standardized social laws in general, we asked?

[handwritten marginal notes: "ref. d", "ref./ref.", ""juvenile"", "to prevent ambiguity", "d", "meaning?", "p."]

(14) The answer? (15) Couldn't this feeling of revolt be curbed, overcome by *t; "have been"*
the offender's parents?

(16) The prevention of juvenile delinquency is not an easy task to under-
take. (17) We saw how much the city, county, state, and even nation[were *(17) needs developing*

Contra-dictary? { doing to help]unfortunate minors overcome their problems and lead new,

useful lives. (18) But the boarding homes, the camps, the schools for cor-

preferably omitted rection are[not helping]to prevent delinquency. (19) The campaign must

begin in the home. (20) The full significance of the parental role must be *empty rhetoric*

realized. *Weak concluding sentence*

Essay II — Critical Comment

This is a moderately good essay with a clear thesis — that parents are to blame for juvenile delinquency — and an ostensibly good source of information; its principal fault is underdevelopment. (I) Though the discussion is intelligent, it lacks sufficient evidence to be convincing. (II) The organization of the essay is good in outline: there is a natural sequence of paragraphs setting up first, the problem and the authority for its answer; second, the answer itself; and third, a general proposal for solving the problem. But in detail the organization is weak: the final clause of the first paragraph ("we began to realize the full scope and gravity of the situation") is completely out of place in this strong rhetorical position, since the idea it contains is never developed in the essay. Sentence 11 should be further supported by details if it is to be really meaningful. In sentence 17 what "we saw" has never been revealed to the reader. The last sentence of the essay is very weak and points to the basic shortcoming of the essay: lack of full development. We want to know exactly what the parents can and should do and exactly how their actions can help solve the problem of delinquency. The whole essay would be improved by the use of concrete illustration. (III) The sentence structure, on the whole, is good (sentence 5, for example, shows the ability to handle a long, complex structure with fluency), but sentences 10 to 15 are something of a muddle. Imprecise pronoun reference leads to the confusing predication of sentence 10 (Can *reasons* — if *these* means reasons — "stem from parents"?) Otherwise most matters of style and mechanics are well handled — there are no errors at all in spelling and no serious errors of punctuation.

••••••

What has been said of essays in the first level applies generally to those in the second except in degree. The same flow of thoughts is to be expected, but it flows less easily. The vocabulary is good but less extensive. Organization and mechanics are usually competently handled. Overall style is mature but with less polish and imagination than in a first-level essay.

It is not unusual in a second-level paper to find in one particular area serious lapses which lower the general quality; for example, it may have excellent content and style but rather poor punctuation.

Essay III

My Favorite Subject

(1) In my four years at high school almost all of my subjects have interested me. (2) But the subject I like the most and which interests me most is history.

(3) Before I was a junior I didn't like history at all. (4) I hoped never to have anything to do with it. (5) But when I became a junior I had to take United States History as a requirement for graduation. (6) I groaned at the thought of history.

subordinate (8) to (7)

became

(7) The first weeks of the course were miserable because I kept telling myself that I didn't like history. (8) My dislike for the course showed in my first quarter's grade. (9) But as the term progressed I[grew]very interested in the subject. (10) The main reason for my growing to like the course was my teacher. (11) She had a way of getting points across as well as making the course interesting.

awkward repetition

logic of (14) explanation needed

(12) I liked the teacher so much and I became so interested in history that when I was a low senior I decided to take a course in California History. (13) The same teacher taught this course. (14) This course, since it dealt with the discovery and development of our state, proved to be even more interesting than the one in United States History.

unnecessary

(15) Now as a high senior I am furthering my study of history by taking Modern History. (16) I only regret that I didn't take this course for a full year instead of just[a]half a year.

unnecessary   (17) When I go to college this fall I hope to continue[on]in the field of

history because there is still so much to learn.   (18) The further study of

history will lead me to one day becoming a history teacher.

Essay III — Critical Comment

There is nothing very good about this paper; on the other hand, there is nothing very bad about it. It is adequate and nothing more. (I) The idea of the essay
is clear: "I like history." But it is far from complete: one wants to know what
it is in the study itself that attracts the writer, but one never finds out. (II) The
organization is mediocre. The introductory paragraph is too short and too bare;
it might well suggest the ideas of sentences 3, 10, and 18. The sequence of ideas
is rather mechanically chronological, though logical and without irrelevancies.
But the statements are not sufficiently developed; just one well-chosen illustration
would probably have gone far to fill in some of the gaps of thought and to breathe
some life into this torpid and unimaginative paper. The concluding paragraph
should be better integrated with the rest of the essay. (III) The paper is free
of grammatical and mechanical errors, though the sentences — like the ideas —
tend to be somewhat over simple and structurally monotonous. In the second
paragraph, for example, every clause uses the *I*-plus verb construction: *I was,
I didn't like, I hoped, I became, I had,* and *I groaned.*

* * * * * *

The most common general characteristic of essays in the third level seems to
be simplicity of both thought and expression. The subject is handled with competence but without distinction; the paragraphs are often short and lack full
development; there is a tendency to write in generalizations without tying them
down to particulars. The organization is usually logical but mechanical, and
transitions are sometimes a problem. Sentence structure and vocabulary are both
usually quite simple, reflecting the quality of the content. The style is wooden.

As a consequence of this general simplicity, few problems of punctuation,
spelling, and sentence structure arise; hence few mistakes are made in these
areas.

Sometimes an essay will be assigned to the third level by a balancing of good
qualities and bad — when, for example, the organization is very poor, but everything else is good.

Essay IV

Rural Life

(1) Life on a farm is full of <u>excitment</u>, hard work, and enjoyment. (2) It *sp.*
takes long hours and hard work to keep a farm in good condition. (3) One has

d   to be a horse doctor, weather <u>bureau</u>, crop expert, and many ∧things all at   ∧*"other"*
once to be able to handle all the problems that come up on the farm. (4) One
has to be able to take <u>dissappointments</u>, discouragement, and <u>dispair</u>.   *sp.*

(5) An average day on a dairy farm usually goes like this: up at 4 or

ref./d   5 A.M. <u>in the morning</u>, a good <u>hardy</u> breakfast, and to work. (6) The cattle   *//str.*
or sp.   are brought in from pasture, milked, and put out again; all the <u>equpment</u> has   *sp.*
to be washed and put away, and the milk stored in a clean, cool place until it

relevancy   is picked up. (7) The milk is then taken to <u>a milk company</u> to be made into
of (7)?   butter, cheese, <u>and so on</u>. (8) Then comes the plowing or harvesting, depend- *d*
ing on what time of year it is. (9) This goes on till lunch and <u>continued</u> after   *t.*
until it's time for milking again. (10) After milking is done, it is supper

time. (11) When supper is over**,** social life begins. (12) Life in the evening is   *comma preferable*
∧*"else"*   pretty much the same as anywhere∧<u>only</u> there is a <u>longer</u> distance to get to   *p./d*
                                                       — *incomplete*
sp.   town or <u>where ever</u> there is to go. (13) There is always something to do on   *comparison*
unity of (12)   a farm. (14) Sometimes in waiting for a calf or colt to be born or maybe a   *(14) frag.*
and (13)   prize bull has pneumonia and the v̶et̶o̶ has been delayed. (15) Idle time is   *and //str*
                                                    (15) weak
rarely found on a farm.   *passive*

trans.   (16) There are many advantages. (17) Some are in seeing animals grow⎤
to what?   and turn into prize stock and seeing fields green and healthy.   ⎦ *develop*

wrong number   (18) Disadvantages are⏜one nevers knows if the ensuing year will bring ⎱ *develop*
p/"that"   success or failure.

Essay IV — Critical Comment

This essay is somewhat less than adequate, but not without merit. (I) The
writer's knowledge of the subject is not in doubt, but not enough of that knowledge is demonstrated. (II) The essay is very unbalanced; the last two "paragraphs" especially are underdeveloped. The second paragraph is better because
it includes more details; but it suffers from the illogical sequence of ideas in its
last four sentences. The opening sentence of the same paragraph is awkward
because of the seemingly gratuitous introduction of *dairy* as a qualifier: surely

this restriction should be made in the introduction or brought in as an example. Finally, the two subjects of the second paragraph — a typical day on a farm and the general busyness of farm life — are not well integrated. (III) There are numerous errors of style and mechanics: the faulty parallelism of sentences 3, 5, and 14; the many errors in spelling; the sloppy structure of sentences 12 and 14. Some sentences, however, are well put together (sentence 6, for example), the whole presentation generally is commendably concrete, and the colloquial style provides authenticity and liveliness appropriate to the subject.

******

Essays in the fourth level tend to show little competence with mechanics; errors of spelling and punctuation appear frequently as well as serious lapses of grammar and sentence structure. These papers are sometimes oversimple, and very typically they show a lack of sustaining power: they begin well with fully developed ideas and accurate sentences, but when the thought begins to fail, the paragraphs become shorter, and the organization and the sentence structure deteriorate. Jerkiness in the thought sequence and a stilted style are common. Such papers not infrequently have flashes of excellence amidst generally poor writing.

Essay V

Juvenile Delinquency

(1) One of the chief causes for juvenile delinquency is not having anything to do. (2) If they had a lot of good places to go & good things to do, then I don't think there would be as much as there is now. (3) In the big cities, the streets are full of big stores and factories, but if they had plenty of recreation halls, then that would be one thing the teenagers could do. (4) People should also encourage the teenagers to take part in sports and other activities --some place they would feel needed. (5) When there is only one movie or show in town and no recreation hall, then there is nothing to do. (6) Teenagers like to keep doing different things. (7) If they keep doing the same thing all the time, then they soon grow tired of it and start looking for something else to do. (8) They don't care whether it's bad or not, all they care about is doing something. (9) Teenagers are very restless people.

(10) Sometimes, in some cases, the parents are at fault. (11) They don't teach their children right from wrong. (12) They should start when the child is very young and teach them then they wouldn't want to do anything wrong.

Marginal annotations:
- str: whose?
- faulty appositive
- red.
- rep.
- red.
- agr./cs
- ref/d/d/p
- what?
- ref/d
-) meaningless
- logic? "little"
-) cs
- for what?
- ref.

d   (13) Parents should also bring their children up in church. (14) It has
been proven that children that have been <u>raised</u> in church,⌈accompanied by
their parents,⌉grow up with a feeling of security and ∧they are very good   *"that"*

X   teenagers. (15) <u>Those kind</u> of teenagers do have something to do--they
have all kinds of church activities to participate in.

(16) I think that if parents <u>wants</u> their children to be good, then they   *agr.*

p   should take them, & go themselves, to church.   *X*

ESSAY V — CRITICAL COMMENT

This is a poor essay, inadequate in almost every respect. (I) It is not devoid
of content, but it is full of unsupported generalizations, at least one of which
(sentence 14) is manifestly not true. The idea with which the student begins
the essay — that teenagers do not have enough to do — is abandoned at the end
of the first paragraph and vaguely reintroduced at the end of the paper. (II)
There is little unity to the essay and no overall organization; it reads as though
the writer were thinking aloud. He wanders aimlessly from a consideration of
recreation facilities through an indictment of parents to a final recommendation
that everyone go to church. The last paragraph has the tone of a summary conclusion, but in fact it summarizes only the last half of the second paragraph.
Very unbalanced, the essay gives no indication of the relative importance of
the ideas suggested: more space is devoted to the first idea than to the others,
but the rhetorical emphasis is on the last idea. (III) There are a great many
gross errors of grammar and sentence structure: the agreement errors of sentences 12 and 16, for example, the faulty apposition of sentence 4, and the pronoun reference errors of sentences 2, 3, and 12. The sentence structure in general
is oversimple and repetitious; particularly noticeable is the repeated *then*-clause
construction.

⁎⁎⁎⁎⁎⁎

Essays in this level typically have numerous gross errors of sentence structure
and punctuation. Vocabulary is weak and inaccurate; diction is usually poor.
Confusion and formlessness are most characteristic of the poorer essays; sense
of structure is lacking; thought is muddled and disorganized. Hence, illogical
constructions, meaningless statements, garbled syntax, and fragmentary sentences are common.

This scale sheet, used in the Cleveland Heights high schools, has been used effectively in the hands of students as a means for noting progress. The sheet is attached to each theme the student hands in so that he has the opportunity to gauge his own work prior to having others read it. When compositions are returned, he sees at once from the scale facets of his work that need strengthening as well as those in which he has improved. Student readers, whether individuals or in committees, find in the scale the general criteria needed to judge intelligently the themes they read.

COMPOSITION RATING SCALE*

Cleveland Heights-University Heights City School District

ASSIGNMENT	STUDENT		DATE
	PURPOSE		

A. Content—50%

Convincing						Unconvincing
persuasive, sincere, enthusiastic, certain						
Organized						Jumbled
logical, planned, orderly, systematic						
Thoughtful						Superficial
reflective, perceptive, probing, inquiring						
Broad						Limited
comprehensive, complete, extensive range of data, inclusive						
Specific						Vague
concrete, definite, detailed, exact						

B. Style—30%

Fluent						Restricted
expressive, colorful,						
Cultivated						Awkward
varied, mature, descriptive, smooth appropriate						

---

*Used in Cleveland Heights-University Heights City School District, Cleveland Heights, Ohio. Used by permission of Leonard Freyman, English-Library Coordinator.

Strong						Weak

effective, striking,
forceful, idioms,
fresh, stimulating

C. Conventions—20%

Correct Writing Form						Incorrect Form

paragraphing, heading,
punctuation, spelling

Conventional Grammar						Substandard

sentence structure,
agreement, references, etc.

Although written primarily for students of college freshman composition, this article will have relevance for high school students, especially in the upper grades. These suggestions are formulated negatively, but we can easily construe their positive counterparts and use them as principles.

HOW TO WRITE AN "F" PAPER*

JOSEPH C. PATTISON

Obscure the Ideas:

1. Select a topic that is big enough to let you wander around the main idea without ever being forced to state it precisely. If an assigned topic has been limited for you, take a detour that will allow you to amble away from it for a while.

2. Pad! Pad! Pad! Do not develop your ideas. Simply restate them in safe, spongy generalizations to avoid the need to find evidence to support what you say. Always point out repetition with the phrase, "As previously noted . . . ." Better yet, repeat word-for-word at least one or two of your statements.

3. Disorganize your discussion. For example, if you are using the time order to present your material, keep the reader alert by making a jump from the past to the present only to spring back into the past preparatory to leap into the future just before the finish of the point about the past. Devise comparable stratagems to use with such other principles for organizing a discussion as space, contrast, cause-effect, and climax.

4. Begin a new paragraph every sentence or two.
    By generous use of white space, make the reader aware that he is looking at a page blank of sustained thought.

    Like this.

Mangle the Sentences

5. Fill all the areas of your sentences with deadwood. Incidentally, "the area of" will deaden almost any sentence, and it is particularly flat when displayed prominently at the beginning of a sentence.

6. Using fragments and run-on or comma-spliced sentences. Do not use a main subject and a main verb, for the reader will get the complete thought too easily. Just toss him part of the idea at a time, as in "Using fragments . . . ." To gain sentence variety, throw in an occasional run-on sentence thus the reader will have to read slowly and carefully to get the idea.

7. Your sentence order invert for statement of the least important matters. That will force the reader to be attentive to understand even the simplest points you make.

---

*Joseph C. Pattison, *College English*, 25, 25 (October 1963), 38-39. Used by permission of Joseph C. Pattison.

8. You, in the introduction, body, and conclusion of your paper, to show that you can contrive ornate, graceful sentences, should use involution. Frequent separation of subjects from verbs by insertion of involved phrases and clauses will prove that you know what can be done to a sentence.

Slovenize the Diction:

9. Add the popular "-wise" and "-ize" endings to words. Say, "Timewise, it is fastest to go by U. S. 40," rather than simply, "It is fastest to go by U. S. 40." Choose "circularize" in preference to "circulate." Practice will smartenize your style.

10. Use vague words in place of precise ones. From the start, establish vagueness of tone by saying, "The thing is . . . ." instead of, "The issue is . . . ." Make the reader be imaginative throughout his reading of your paper.

11. Employ lengthy Latinate locutions wherever possible. Shun the simplicity of style that comes from apt use of short, old, familiar words, especially those of Anglo-Saxon origin. Show that you can get the maximum (L.), not mere the most (AS.), from every word choice you make.

12. Inject humor into your writing by using the wrong word occasionally. Write "then" when you mean "than" or "to" when you mean "too." Every reader likes a laugh.

13. Find a "tried and true" phrase to use to clinch a point. It will have a comfortingly folksy sound for the reader. Best of all, since you want to end in a conversational and friendly way, sprinkle your conclusion with clichés. "Put a little frosting on the cake," as the saying goes.

Well, too ensconce this whole business in a nutshell, you, above all, an erudite discourse on nothing in the field of your topic should pen. Thereby gaining the reader's credence in what you say.

Suggestion-wise, one last thing: file-ize this list for handy reference the next time you a paper write.